Knowledge Maturing

Creating learning rich workplaces for agile organisations

The MATURE Consortium

This report is based on the research conducted within the European Integrating Project MATURE (http://mature-ip.eu) between April 2008 and May 2012. The project was co-funded by the European Commission under the 7th Framework Programme ICT under contract no. 216359.

FZI Research Center for Information Technologies, Karlsruhe, Germany
Prof. Dr. Andreas Schmidt (Scientific Coordinator)

CIMNE, Barcelona, Spain
Pablo Franzolini (Administrative Coordinator)

Graz University of Technology, Austria
Prof. Dr. Stefanie Lindstaedt

SAP AG, Karlsruhe, Germany
Dr. Uwe Riss

University of Innsbruck, Austria
Prof. Dr. Ronald Maier

London Metropolitan University, LTRI, UK
Prof. Dr. John Cook

University of Paderborn, Germany
Prof. Dr. Johannes Magenheim

University of Applied Sciences Northwestern Switzerland
Prof. Dr. Knut Hinkelmann

Pontydysgu, Pontybridd, UK
Graham Attwell

University of Warwick, UK
Prof. Dr. Jenny Bimrose, Prof. Dr. Alan Brown

BOC Asset Management GmbH, Vienna, Austria
Dr. Robert Woitsch

Structuralia, Madrid, Spain
Eduardo Car

Contributors

EDITORS

Andreas P. Schmidt, Karlsruhe University of Applied Sciences
andreas_peter.schmidt@hs-karlsruhe.de   http://andreas.schmidt.name

Christine Kunzmann, Kompetenzorientierte Personalentwicklung
kontakt@christine-kunzmann.de   http://christine-kunzmann.de

MAIN AUTHORS

Andreas Kaschig, University of Innsbruck

Alexander Sandow, University of Innsbruck

Ronald Maier, University of Innsbruck

Andreas Schmidt, Karlsruhe University of Applied Sciences

OTHER AUTHORS

Sally-Anne Barnes, University of Warwick

Jenny Bimrose, University of Warwick

Simone Braun, FZI Research Center for Information Technologies

Alan Brown, University of Warwick

John Cook, Learning Technologies Research Institute, London Metropolitan University

Knut Hinkelmann, University of Applied Sciences Northwestern Switzerland

Michael Kohlegger, University of Innsbruck

Tobias Ley, Talinn University

Johannes Magenheim, University of Paderborn

Athanasios Mazarakis, FZI Research Center for Information Technologies

Tobias Nelkner, University of Paderborn

Andrew Ravenscroft, University of East London

Uwe Riss, SAP AG

Barbara Thönssen, University of Applied Sciences Northwestern Switzerland

Hans-Friedrich Witschel, University of Applied Sciences Northwestern Switzerland

Contents

1
Why is knowledge maturing important for you?

The agility of organizations has become the critical success factor for competitiveness in a world characterized by an accelerating rate of change. Agility requires that companies and their employees together and *mutually dependently* learn and develop their competencies efficiently in order to improve productivity of knowledge work. As a reaction to failures of organisation-driven approaches to technology-enhanced learning and the success of community-driven approaches in the spirit of Web 2.0, we have recently seen a paradigm shift in technology support for learning towards more participatory approaches in which learners are seen as active contributors. Within enterprises, this new perspective brings together traditionally separated disciplines like e-learning, knowledge management, and human resources development, but also requires a fundamental change of the culture of the respective enterprise towards an enterprise 2.0, which is characterized by enhanced collaboration and a cultural of employee participation.

These developments are at the heart of how individuals and companies value and deal with knowledge. To make sense it and to productively shape the change process, we need a new conceptual framework that is both well-grounded on extensive research and pratically relevant and proven through application in numerous projects. The Knowledge Maturing perspective is a novel approach that helps understanding the fundamental change, the barriers and disruptions in knowledge development, but also shows opportunities and gives guidance to make use of them.

2

Describing Knowledge Maturing: The Knowledge Maturing Phase Model

Knowledge maturing describes the development of knowledge from a team, community, or organisational perspective. It can be divided into distinct phases along which the characteristics of learning and dealing with knowledge change significantly. The Knowledge Maturing Phase Model can be used to analyse and understand real-world knowledge maturing practices and helps to distinguish between different problem areas and suitable solutions.

2.1   CONCEPT

Knowledge maturing is based on the assumption that learning is an inherently social and collaborative activity in which individual learning processes are interdependent and dynamically interlinked with each other: the output of one learning process is input to the next. If we have a look at this phenomenon from a distance, we can observe a knowledge flow across different interlinked individual learning processes. Knowledge becomes less contextualized, more explicitly linked, easier to communicate, in short: it matures.

2.1.1   Definition

We define **knowledge maturing** as the goal-oriented development of collective knowledge, or better as goal-oriented learning on a collective level where

- **goal-oriented** describes knowledge maturing as a process with a direction. The goal can be an individual goal (e.g., deepen understanding in an area out of curiosity), a team goal (e.g., grasp known errors with respect to a product that the team works on), or an organisational goal (e.g., refine an organisations core competency). Goals typically change over time and get aligned in social processes, resulting in a direction as a (mostly a posteriori) interpretation.

- **collective level** can refer to different levels of granularity, e.g., a team, an organisation or a community. Knowledge maturing is not the result of an individual's activity, but of an interconnected series of activities of interacting individuals, frequently also within different collectives.

- **knowledge** is understood as both cognitive structures bound to individuals' minds (becoming manifest in their behaviour) and as an abstraction of the knowledge of individuals in a collective.

2.1.2 Phases of Knowledge Maturing

When having a closer look at how knowledge maturing takes, we discover a wealth of different forms of knowledge and learning. Knowledge maturing can be described by dividing knowledge maturing into distinct phases:

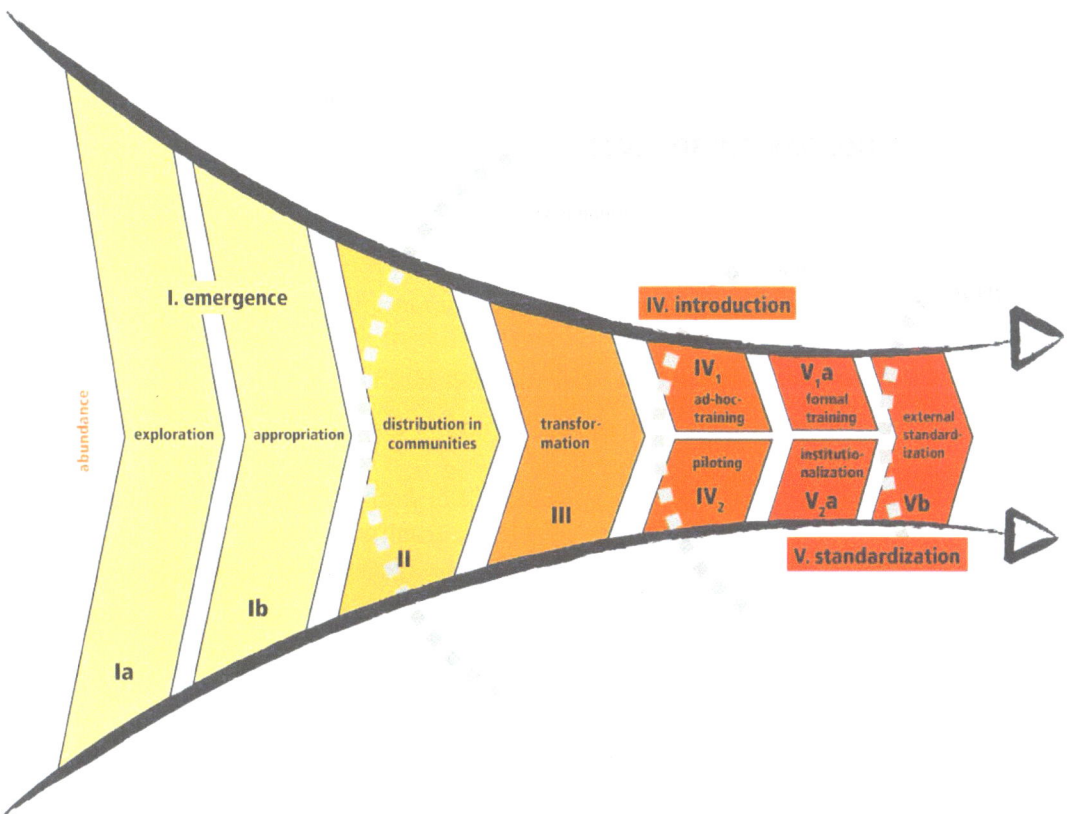

Figure 1: The Knowledge Maturing Phase Model

- **I. Emergence.** Individuals create personal knowledge by pursuing their interests in browsing abundant knowledge spaces inside and beyond the organisation, opening up for new knowledge and the changes it might bring about. Based on the findings of our studies, we revised this phase to include two subphases, exploration and appropriation.

  - **Ia. Exploration:** New knowledge is developed by individuals either in highly informal discussions or by browsing the knowledge spaces available inside the organisation and beyond. Extensive search and retrieval activities often result in loads of material influencing creative processes of idea generation. Knowledge is subjective, deeply embedded in the originator's context and the vocabulary used for communication might be vague and restricted to the originator.

  - **Ib. Appropriation:** New knowledge or results found in the investigation phase that have been enriched, refined or otherwise contextualized with respect to their use are now appropriated by the individual, i.e. personalised and contributions are marked so that an individual can benefit from its future (re-)use. While many

9

initiatives for knowledge management have focused on sharing knowledge or even detaching knowledge from humans as "media", at least in a more individualistic culture, individuals also require support for appropriation.

- **II. Distribution (community interaction):** The first phase on the level of communities describes interactions between individuals driven by social motives and the benefits that individuals typically attribute to sharing knowledge. These are, among others, belonging to a preferred social group, thus increasing the probability of getting back knowledge from the community when one needs it. Distribution is not meant in the sense of a one way street of individuals contributing new knowledge that they have committed to. The phase includes discussing the new knowledge, negotiating its meaning and impact, co-developing knowledge, convincing others and agreeing plus committing to the knowledge as collective. From the perspective of semantics, a common terminology is developed and shared among community members.

- **III. Transformation:** Artefacts created in the preceding phases are often inherently unstructured and still highly subjective and embedded in the community context which means they are only comprehensible for people in this community due to shared knowledge needed to interpret them. Transformation means that knowledge is restructured and put into a form appropriate for moving it across the community's boundaries. Structured documents are created in which knowledge is de-subjectified, sometimes formalized using established containers and context is made explicit to ease the transfer to collectives other than the originating community.

- **IV. Introduction**: Knowledge is prepared with a specific focus on enhancing understandability, handed on and applied in an ad-hoc manner in trainings in which a selected group of users is instructed using didactically prepared material. We found two primary interpretations of introduction, (1) an instructional setting called ad-hoc training and (2) an experimental setting called piloting.

    - **IV$_1$. Ad-hoc training:** Documents produced in the preceding phase are typically not well suited as learning materials because no didactical considerations were taken into account. Now the topic is refined to improve comprehensibility in order to ease its consumption or re-use. Individual learning objects are arranged to cover a broader subject area. Tests allow to determine the knowledge level and to select learning objects or learning paths.

    - **IV$_2$. Piloting:** Typically, not every implementation detail can be foreseen in the preceding phase. Knowledge is arranged in a way so that it can be applied in a dedicated, specific experiment involving not only the creators of knowledge, but other stakeholders. Experiences are collected with a test case before a larger roll-out of a product, a service to an external user community, e.g., customers or stakeholders, or new organisational rules, procedures or processes to an organisational-internal target community such as project teams, work groups, subsidiaries or other organisational units.

- **V. Standardization**: The knowledge is further solidified and formally established in the organization to be used in repeatable formal trainings, work practices, processes, products or services. As in phase IV, we distinguish an instructional setting with standardised training activities, called formal training, and an experimental setting turning pilots into standard organizational infrastructure, processes and practices, called institutionalisation. The term standard, finally, also evoked the connotation of external standardisation initiatives which are similar for both settings, transcend the organizational boundaries and move knowledge maturing to the level of societies.

- **V₁a. Formal training:** In an instructional setting, the subject area becomes teachable to novices. A curriculum integrates learning content into a sequence using sophisticated didactical concepts in order to guide learners in their learning journeys to capture a subject area thus increasing the probability of successful knowledge transfer. Learning objects are arranged into courses covering a broader subject area. Learning modules and courses can be further combined into programs used for preparing for taking on a new role or for career development.

- **V₂a. Institutionalisation:** In the organisation-internal case, formalised documents that have been learned by knowledge workers are solidified and implemented into the organisational infrastructure in the form of processes, business rules and/or standard operating procedures. In the organisation-external case, products or services are launched on the market. They are institutionalised into the portfolio of products and services offered by the organisation.

- **Vb. External standardisation:** The ultimate maturity sub-phase is very similar for both paths, the instructional and the experimental path, and covers some form of standardisation or certification. On an individual level, certificates confirm that participants of formal trainings achieved a certain degree of proficiency. On an organisational level, certificates allow organisations to prove compliance with a set of rules that they have agreed to fulfil, e.g., with service level agreements or regulations such as Basel II or SOX. Concerning products and services, certificates show compliance to laws, regulations or recommendations that can, should or must be fulfilled before a product or service can be offered in a certain market.

This model describes characteristic phases of knowledge maturing, but does not imply a linear development that is the same in each and every case. Therefore, *this model should not be misunderstood as a process model in the business process modelling sense*. Rather we can observe complex patterns like the combination of knowledge assets, backward steps and cycles as well as improvement patterns.

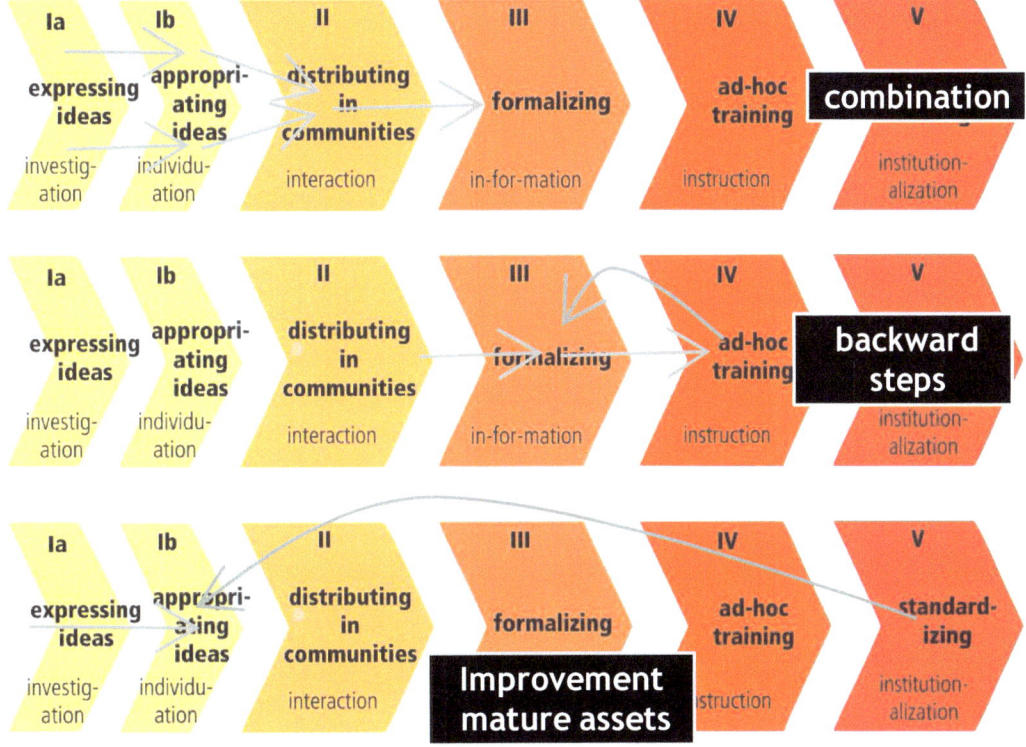

The phase model allows for some interesting observations and insights about knowledge maturing:

- When it comes to individual learning, formal learning seems to be more appropriate for the later phases (i.e., more mature knowledge), e.g., courses, classes, textbooks. It can leverage the decontextualization and well-structuredness through standardized approaches that efficiently target novices to the knowledge area. On the other end, informal learning plays a much bigger role as there are no materials that are associated with formal learning. Due to the high degree of contextualization, individuals require deep background knowledge that is usually associated with experts.

- In earlier phases, knowledge development is typically driven by interests of individuals and teams, while in later phases clearer goals exist in an organization, particularly when it comes to implementation and standardization.

- Both of these observations also help to explain discontinuities on the organizational level. Ad-hoc training is under the responsibility of HR development or training departments (where the instructional perspective dominates), learning in the formalization phase is managed by the operating departments themselves where self-organized knowledge is more the dominating paradigm.

2.2 PRACTICAL RELEVANCE

The Knowledge Maturing Phase Model allows for analysing concrete families of knowledge processes in companies, diagnose its problems and propose possible solutions. This can be illustrated by examples that we have collected in researching and applying the model in practical projects:

- An interview of the study we conducted in MATURE related the knowledge maturing phase model to his company's experience and found that the "distribution in communities" (phase II) was not required because within his company, this does not play a role. Within the course of the interview, it was found that the company has implemented a continuous improvement programme. Employees are asked to put new ideas into an idea management system in a structured description format. These ideas (mostly from individuals) are then assessed by an expert panel. "Good" ideas get rewards. The interviewee expressed his experience that they do not have a problem with idea generation because way too many ideas are generated, which are frequently of little use to the company because they are too trivial. n terms of the knowledge maturing phase model, the company expected employees to jump directly from appropriation to formalization. This omits the crucial phase of discussing ideas in a group of people with a shared context. Typically, within this phase individual contributions are amalgamated to larger ideas that are better understood and more developed. Such a discussion is not just a simple selection process (like the expert panel, which would be the filtering function between phase III and IV), but also a co-creation phase in which team members build upon the results of others.

- In a consulting project for a large German financial services company, the company was dealing with the question which software product to select for their "collaboration" needs inside their IT services unit. They asked for external advice whether a collaboration platform such as Microsoft Sharepoint or a wiki-based solution would be more appropriate. At the beginning of the consulting process, the knowledge maturing phase model was introduced to clarify the collaboration problems that needed to be addressed. As a result of a reflection process, they have found out that they actually have two different collaboration "problems", each of them located in different maturity phases. On the one side, they collaborate with external partners to co-create new solutions, on the other side, they need to systematically manage their subcontractors so that everyone has access to the latest contract version and to contractually relevant deliverables. While the first situation is located in phase II (distribution in communities), the second is located in phase V2a (institutionalization) and Vb (external standardization), mostly referring to company standards for contract management, but some of this is also relevant for external compliance aspects). While both problems are related to the same activities (communicate with people, co-develop artifacts), it is important to realize that the characteristics are different. The first situation needs quick and easy collaboration (changeability) where structure can easily get into the way, the second situation needs traceability, clearly defined access rights, among others, i.e., stability with respect to rules and structure.

- While it is generally desirable to aim at a balanced distribution of knowledge maturing processes, companies are not free to choose where they operate. There are external regulations, particularly in the medical sectors, that require a high degree of standardization when it comes to the production of medical equipment. The production processes need to be certified in an expensive procedure, and compliance to the certified processes need to be documented. This can lead to situations in which a company still needs to manufacture according to processes which are known to be less efficient than newer production processes so that employees can see their idea come to practical applications only after a considerable time period (usually at least three, but up to ten years). This creates motivational issues to stay innovative, which is needed to retain the competitive advantage. A company that has been interviewed as part of LBS has realized the problems that are associated with such conditions and introduced (a) a highly attractive incentive system with considerable benefits, and (b) an experimentation environment as part of a "rapid response team" that is very well equipped with new technology and is responsible for rapid prototyping for new customer requests. This makes sure that employees are motivated to develop new ideas and they can experience them getting applied at least at prototyping stage early on without interfering with external compliance requirements.

2.3   IN-DEPTH CONSIDERATIONS AND SCIENTIFIC CONTEXT

The notion of knowledge that underlies the knowledge maturing phase model can be characterized by the differentiation in *cognifacts*, i.e. individual knowledge, expertise, and competencies, sociofacts, i.e. collective knowledge phenomena (including collective rules, norms, structures of social interaction, but particularly also collective knowledge in the narrower sense, and artefacts, i.e. codified representations of knowledge.

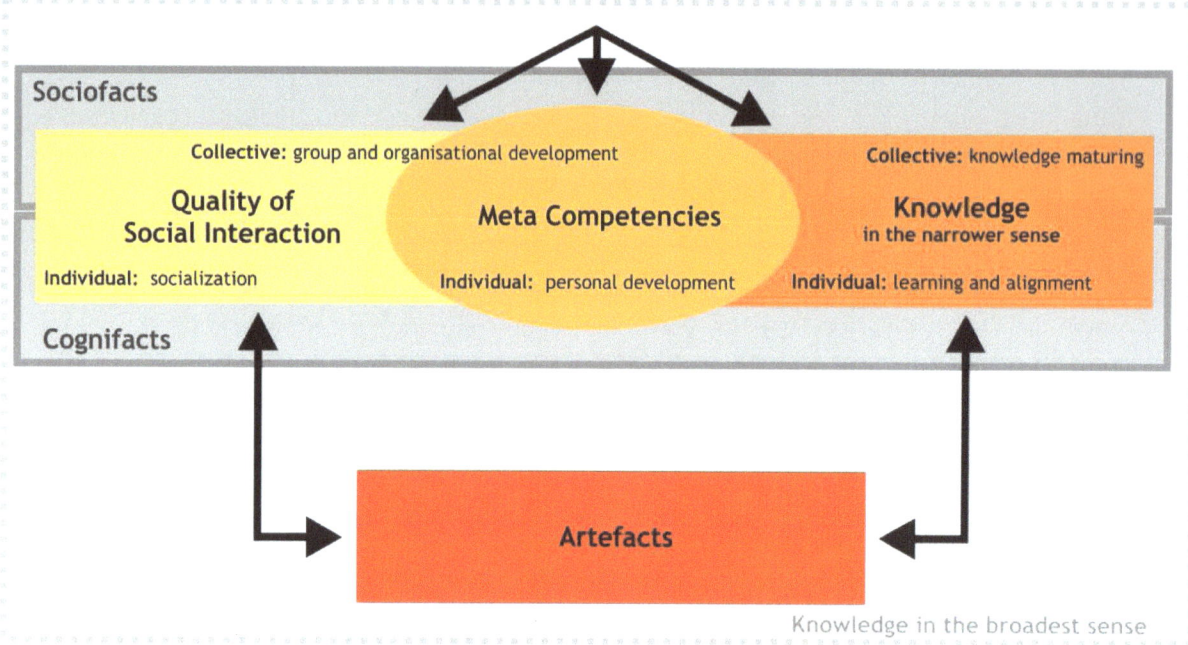

Figure 3: Dimensions of knowledge maturing

- The **knowledge** dimension refers to knowledge in a narrow sense, i.e., domain knowledge in a non-tangible form, including "know-what" and "know-how" which is always bound to people's minds while everything beyond that is an *abstraction*. That means that we have to distinguish:

  o **Individual** level. Knowledge is bound to individuals' minds and their structures. The process of augmenting and changing that knowledge is what is usually called (individual) **learning** processes.

  o **Collective** level. This level is an abstraction if we "zoom out" from an individual to a (larger) group of people. Collective knowledge is an aggregation of individual pieces of knowledge. From this meso- or macro-level[1], we can see if an individual learning process contributes to an advancement of the collective knowledge level in line with organisational goals which is what we call **knowledge maturing**. While learning at an individual level is always the prerequisite for any advancement on the collective level, there is a fundamental difference if an individual just learns what others have learnt before or if this learning is an active construction process that advances knowledge on a higher level. We call this "higher level" the collective level. This has a quality of its own while still acknowledging that it is an abstraction from the sum of individual knowledge.

- **Artefacts** are manifestations, touchable or visible items, either in physical or electronic form (e.g., models, documents, videos, notes), that have been directly or indirectly created by humans. While those artefacts do not "contain knowledge" in the proper sense, they are instruments to communicate about knowledge and mediate its development, are involved in learning processes and thus reflect some aspect of maturity of knowledge. The maturity of artefacts depends on the maturity of the underlying knowledge, but not vice versa. Very

---

[1] Depending on the size of the organisational unit (macro stands for the entire organisation, e.g., a company, whereas meso denotes any organisational level within, e.g., a work group, a project or a department.

14

mature knowledge does not need to have corresponding artefacts. A **maturing process for artefacts** needs to be clearly distinguished from knowledge maturing, but is dependent on the knowledge maturing process and might even influence the latter.

- Not only artefacts facilitate learning and knowledge maturing, but also **"meta-competencies"** of the individual or the organisation.

  o **Individual level.** As knowledge maturing rarely is an individual activity, but rather a collaborative activity where individual activities become interconnected, the individuals in that process need collaboration competencies that enable them to participate in knowledge maturing. This comprises a general willingness and competencies to interact with others, communicate, negotiate, compromise and accept rules, learning and coping strategies. These determine the capability and affect the motivation to engage in maturing activities. Evolution of these competencies is what we call **personal development**.

  o **Collective level.** An organisation's capability to make knowledge maturing happen within its social system refers to organisational competencies like innovation and change to external stimuli, communicative culture, dealing with errors, work organisation etc. Evolution of these competencies is part of **team** and **organisational development**.

- **Quality of social interaction** refers to more stable areas like the value system, non-explicit rules and norms. On the **collective level**, an evolution of this is part **of team and organisation development** processes, while on the **individual level** we call this process **socialization**.

As knowledge maturing is an inherently social phenomenon, it has turned out to be useful to describe it from a symbolic interactionism (Blumer, 1969) point of view. The result is a categorization of knowledge (in its broadest sense): **Artefacts** refer to codified representations of knowledge, **cognifacts** refer to individual knowledge, expertise, and competencies, and **sociofacts** describe collective knowledge (including collective rules, norms, but also collective knowledge in the narrower sense).

2.4   FURTHER READING

Kaschig, A., Maier, R., Sandow, A., Schmidt, A., Thalmann, S. (Eds.): D1.1 Results of the Ethnographic Study and Conceptual Knowledge Maturing Model, Deliverable 1.1 of the FP7 IP MATURE, Section 5, http://d.mature-ip.eu/D1.1

Kaschig, A., Maier, R., Sandow, A. & Schmidt, A. (Eds.) (2010). D1.2 - Results Of The Representative Study And Refined Conceptual Knowledge Maturing Model. Deliverable of the FP7 IP MATURE, Section 5, http://d.mature-ip.eu/D1.2

Kaschig, A., Maier, R., Sandow, A. & Schmidt, A. (Eds.) (2011). D1.3 Results of In-depth Case Studies, Recommendations and Final Knowledge Maturing Model. Deliverable of the FP7 IP MATURE, Section 5, http://d.mature-ip.eu/D1.3

Schmidt, Andreas (2005). Knowledge Maturing and the Continuity of Context as a Unifying Concept for Knowledge Management and E-Learning. In: Proceedings of I-KNOW 05, Graz, Austria. http://publications.andreas.schmidt.name/IKNOW05_aschmidt.pdf

Maier, Ronald, Schmidt, Andreas (2007). Characterizing Knowledge Maturing: A Conceptual Process Model for Integrating E-Learning and Knowledge Management. In: Gronau, Norbert (eds.): 4th Conference Professional Knowledge Management - Experiences and Visions (WM '07), Potsdam,

GITO, pp. 325-334
http://publications.andreas.schmidt.name/Maier_Schmidt_KnowledgeMaturing_WM07.pdf

Maier, Ronald, Schmidt, Andreas (under review). Knowledge Maturing Model: Explaining Organizational Knowledge Creation Based on User-Generated Content and Social Networks. Submitted to Knowledge Management Research & Practice

3

Contributing to Knowledge Maturing: Identifying Activities

Knowledge Maturing Activities describe activities of individuals and teams as key elements for knowledge maturing within organisations. Their identification helps to analyse and prioritise which activities need more or other forms of support.

3.1 CONCEPT

The attempt to pack and articulate organizational Knowledge Maturing Activities (KMA) in context of creating learning rich workplaces led to a study crossing theoretical definition as well as practical validation. The performance of activities identified contribute to the development of knowledge on a collective level, where usually the goal-oriented learning of individuals involved goes way beyond in its effects.

The concept of activity proves to be beneficial to analyse knowledge maturing where the perspective of practice finds its roots in knowledge work in different professions, positions and industries. Practices formed by individuals or teams are characterised by knowledge work comprising activities of acquisition, creation, collection, organization, maintenance, systemization, communication and application of knowledge. Primarily, the exploration and joint creation of knowledge is operationalized as strategic focus and applied to all business processes. It is for KMAs to facilitate communication, function as mediation or as cognitive support, making use of artefacts, cognifacts and sociofacts (see section 2) as well as producing such for business progress.

In preparation to the empirical study on deriving an agreed list of KMA occurring across the whole of knowledge maturing processes, the profound theoretical investigation was supplemented by an ethnographically-informed study to match elaborated KMA to real-world maturing practices and activities. The scope of organisations investigated widened the picture of perception by underlying companies of different size, sector and knowledge intensity. What resulted was a comprehensive and practically corresponding list of twelve KMAs (see **Fehler! Verweisquelle konnte nicht gefunden werden.**), discussed and formulated on grounds of deep understanding of activities performed by knowledge workers and used as interview guideline to the empirical study.

1	**Find relevant digital resources**	*Search for information, e.g. documents, web pages or images.*
2	**Embed information at individual or organisational level**	*Include the information into one's own knowledge base, which could be a (personal or shared) file system, a (personal/team/corporate) wiki, or similar.*
3	**Keep up-to-date with organisation-related knowledge**	*Making sure that oneself or another person stays up-to-date regarding a certain topic*
4	**Familiarise oneself with new information**	*Making oneself familiar with e.g. a topic or a community or processes*
5	**Reorganise information at individual or organisational level**	*Restructure collections (file systems, wikis, …), consolidate different approaches to collective structuring, removing outdated items, improving findability through assigning metadata, "gardening" of wikis, vocabularies etc., rearrange contents or files, clean-up work spaces and assure quality of a collection of digital resources*
6	**Reflect on and refine work practices or processes**	*This reflects process maturing from discovery of task or process patterns, the analysis thereof to improving practices and/or processes. The knowledge maturing activity thus comprises practices (i.e. not formally specified), procedures (informal or endorsed) as well as processes (specified, defined)*
7	**Create and co-develop digital resources**	*Generate new or update existing contents by oneself or together with others.*
8	**Share and release digital resources**	*Share denotes the informal, release the formal or official part of granting access to contents for a specified or unspecified group of people.*
9	**Restrict access and protect digital resources**	*Restricting access to contents.*
10	**Find people with particular knowledge or expertise**	*Identify a contact person, e.g. by skills*
11	**Communicate with people**	*interact with others, e.g. face-to-face, by phone, by mail*
12	**Assess, verify and rate information**	*Evaluate contents with respect to certain quality criteria like accurateness, up-to-dateness, usefulness or people with respect to their capacities or behaviour*

Table 1: List of Knowledge Maturing Activities

In the large scale interview study, the listed KMAs were investigated with respect to three concepts: "perceived importance", "perceived support" and "perceived success". 139 interviewees were asked to reflect on how important they think that the KMAs were for increasing maturity of knowledge in the organisation they represent, how far organisational or ICT instruments contribute to these knowledge maturing activities and finally, the interviewees were asked to state on how successfully they believe these KMAs are performed in their organisation. Besides rating on each proposed KMA, the respondents were asked to provide further KMAs performed in their organisation (see section 3.2).

The results brought up relatively high mean values to all three concepts, having the interviewees predominantly agree with the worked out KMAs under the presented aspects.

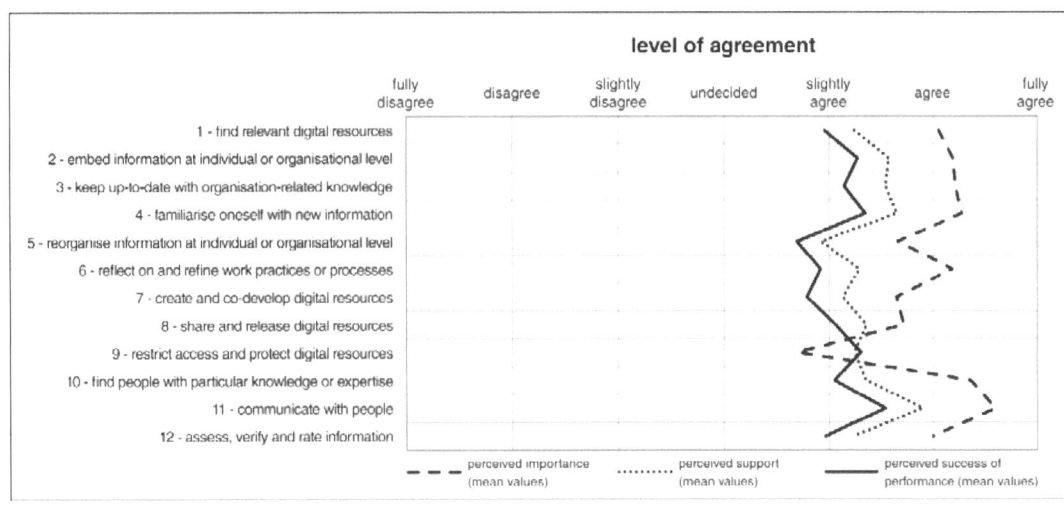

Figure 4: Importance, Support and Success of Performance of KMAs

Further interesting facets to the concepts are to highlight:

- **Perceived importance:** Medians indicate that at least 50% of respondents agreed or fully agreed that all of the twelve KMAs are important for increasing KM in their organization. The agreement to the importance of KMAs *"find relevant digital resources"*, *"reflect on and refine work practices or processes"*, *"find people with particular knowledge or expertise"* and *"communicate with people"* was even higher, as for at least 50% of the respondents fully agreed. The KMA with the highest standard deviation (2.15) is *"restrict access and protect digital resources"*. Frequencies make believe that two different interpretations of that particular KMA might exist.

- **Perceived support:** The agreement to the statement that the respective KMA is supported in the respondents' organisations is not as high as the agreement of perceived importance to the same KMA. However, for ten out of twelve KMAs the median proved to have at least 50% of interviewees agree or fully agree to aids at place. With respect to the KMA *"reorganise information at individual or organisational level'* 66.4% and with respect to *"assess, verify and rate information"* 69.9% of interviewees slightly agreed, agreed or fully agreed. Again, the most heterogeneous answers were given to the KMA *"restrict access and protect digital resources"* (standard deviation is 1.81).

- **Perceived success of performance:** Compared to the agreement to perceived support of KMAs, the level of agreement of interviewees hereto is again lower. Nevertheless, more than 50% of interviewees (exact values after each activity) agreed or fully agreed that the KMAs *"familiarise oneself with new information"* (54.4%), *"share and release digital resources"* (51.2%), *"restrict access and protect digital resources"* (61.0%), *"find people with particular knowledge or expertise"* (52.4%) and *"communicate with people"* (58.7%) are performed successfully in their organisation. With respect to the remaining seven out of twelve KMAs, a median of five indicates that at least 50% of respondents slightly agreed, agreed or fully agreed.

Generally, the constituted list of KMAs was found to be important for increasing knowledge maturity in interviewee's organisations. Moreover, mean values of given answers decrease from aspect to aspect, which noticeably indicate that the approved KMA are actually less supported than the interviewees necessitate and also explains the even lower ratings of successful KMA performances by now.

3.2 PRACTICAL RELEVANCE

Tools for supporting knowledge maturing support individuals in their activities that contribute to knowledge maturing. The variety of workplace activities makes it usually difficult to judge where support is most needed. The Knowledge Maturing Activities represent a proven selection and categorization of activities that can form the basis for diagnosing which elements of work practices are not well supported. Furthermore, the empirical results provide guidance which activities are usually considered more critical than others.

On a more detailed level, the characteristics of Knowledge Maturing Activities change in the various phases. This insight is a key aspect guiding how to support knowledge maturing. Functions of IT systems primarily target at supporting activities, and this support needs to be aware of the phase characteristics. We illustrate this with the three activities that have been found to be highly important, but not well supported and performed in the LSS: (6) reflect on and refine work practices and processes, (10) find people with particular knowledge or expertise, and (12) assess, verify and rate information, which at the same time also correspond to different strands of knowledge: knowledge how to do something (process), knowledge about others (people), and knowledge in artefacts (content).

Find people with particular knowledge or expertise. In phases Ia and Ib, others are mainly a source for inspiration. Quick and easy access, i.e. low effort for contacting and shared context, is most important. Also, awareness of others' activities frequently triggers interactions instead of planned search for a specific topic. Phase II is about community formation and ensuring their sustainability. While a shared context is still important to ensure mutual understanding, more targeted searching for other individuals takes place, still based on informal keywords, which is also based on a deepened understanding developed in phase I. In the transforming phase (III), with the vocabulary more widely agreed, the possibility of using a shared vocabulary can be exploited, e.g., for assisting staffing decisions or employee directories. For phases IV and Va, systematic approaches to human resource development such as succession planning, competence and talent management are the primary instruments that allow for finding internal and external persons; notions of "competency" and "potential" for future acquisition of "competency" replace more informal notions of "topics" or "interests" for describing individuals' capabilities. Finally, the standardization phase (Vb), focuses comparability of individuals: standardized qualifications, certificates and the regulatory environment affecting their use are the primary instruments to guide finding people.

Reflect on and refine practices or processes. the early phases deal with exploring possibilities and getting inspiration from external sources (Ia) and incorporating the results into one's own practice, revisiting the effects and deciding on modifications (Ib). Typically, this involves personal task management. In phase II, work practice and related experiences are shared with others, and commonalities are distilled during reflection in teams. In phase III, this is transformed into, e.g., good practices and other how-to documents, often already initial process models which are still descriptive in nature and the result of structured collective reflection. In phase IV, the process models are transferred beyond the boundaries of the collective in which they have been created and used to pilot a certain approach in a specific area, and in phase Va to roll it out to the whole company or organization. Process models are now used in a prescriptive way, e.g., by implementing parts of the processes as part of IT tools. Key performance indicators are used as a basis for reflection. Finally, in phase Vb, processes are standardized across companies. The notion of compliance to external regulations, certification of organizations adhering to standardized processes as well as formal training (Va) and certification (Vb) of employees for being proficient with the standardized processes become important.

Assess, verify, and rate information. In phases I and II, content artefacts are mainly rated (and individuals access ratings) through informal instruments, such as implicit rating relevance through tagging, five-star methods and organizing artefacts in collections. In phase III, typically more elaborate criteria for assessment are developed. The later phases introduce more formal

20

assessment processes where quality guidelines are followed, and organizations endorse artefacts as official. Finally, artefacts might be subjected to a standardization process across companies in order to facilitate their application beyond the organisational boundaries.

3.3 IN-DEPTH CONSIDERATIONS AND SCIENTIFIC CONTEXT

Based on the results above, detailed analysis then mapped the three concepts of KMAs to portfolios. Concerning possible KM services, better insight to KMA enhancement was mainly to derive thereby. As for the importance of KMAs is shown to be very high by the empirical study, one can conclude that improving actual practices of knowledge work leads to improved organisational learning and knowledge dissemination. Employees are nevertheless involved in social processes of mutual engagement and shared repertoires, where every data gatherer, knowledge user and knowledge builder can contribute to the whole of organisational competitive advantages when KMA support is at place.

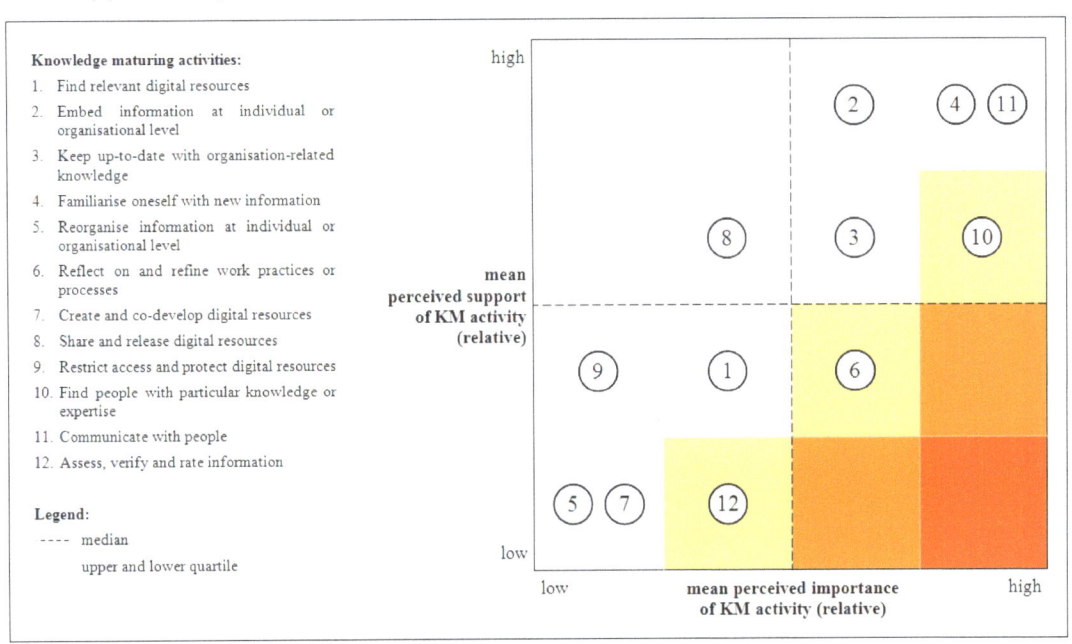

Figure 5: KMA portfolio support – success of performance

In order to elaborate potential KMA support, it is of interest to identify KMAs that are, firstly, deemed important for increasing knowledge maturity, but perceived less supported and, secondly, deemed important, but perceived less successfully performed. In such cases, KM services could be (further) developed to enhance the support of such activities aiming at a more successful performance in organisations. Investigations to this area of interest had the portfolios created, evaluated and presented (Figure 5 and Figure 6)

Eventually, the coloured background of the resulting portfolio underlines which activities are most worthy to focus supportive functionalities on. Considerations are implicated by the different shades representing the norm strategy of activity investment: the higher the perceived importance and the lower the perceived support, the darker the background colour and the higher the lack of software or services to support the KMA.

Relatively to others, the KMAs (4) *"familiarise oneself with new information"*, (11) *"communicate with people"* and (10) *"find people with particular knowledge or expertise"* are deemed most important for increasing knowledge maturity in respondent's organisations. The latter out of this group is less supported and therefore most interesting to enhance aiding functionalities. The KMAs (2) *"embed information at individual or organisational level"*, (3) *"keep up-to-date with organisation-related knowledge"* and (6) *"reflect on and refine work practices or processes"* are deemed of secondary importance, where again the latter KMA is deemed less supported. Additionally, this activity is the only one to the portfolio which belongs to both, the 50 percent of KMAs that are deemed more important and the 50 percent of KMAs that are deemed less supported than others. Hence, *"6-reflect on and refine work practices or processes"* is highly considered to the area of interest. With respect to perceived importance, the KMAs *"1-find relevant digital resources"*, *"8-share and release digital resources"* and *"12-assess, verify and rate information"* fall into a third sub-group, where the least supported could also use facilitation by software or services. The sub-group deemed least important in comparison to other KMAs contains *"5-reorganise information at individual or organisational level"*, *"7-create and co-develop digital resources"* and *"9-restrict access and protect digital resources"*.

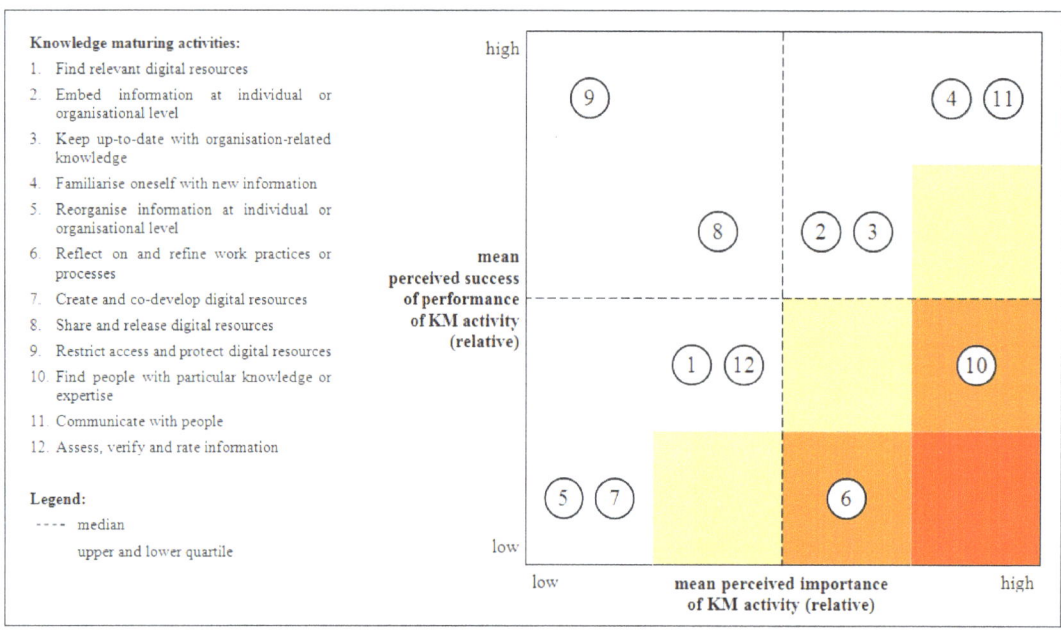

Figure 6: KMA portfolio importance – success of performance

The portfolio matching KMAs of interviewees perceived importance to perceived success of performance in their organisations (Figure 6), proves *"10-find people with particular knowledge or expertise"* and *"6-reflect on and refine work practices or processes"* to be the most interesting activities for functional improvement. The former falls into the group of most important KMAs and, at the same time, is part of the 50 percent of KMAs that are performed less successfully. The latter is deemed to be one of the 50 percent more important KMAs but perceived as one of the three less successfully performed.

Comparing the two portfolios has one conclude that the KMAs *"6-reflect on and refine work practices or processes"* and *"10-find people with particular knowledge or expertise"* are of highest interest for improving their attributive practices of knowledge work. *"12-Assess, verify and rate information"* could also be considered interesting, as for the KMA it is one of the least supported and less successfully performed activities. Even *"1-find relevant digital resources"*, *"5-reorganise information at individual or organisational level"* and *"7-create and co-develop digital resources"* might not be left out when investing in new software or services according to KMA support. In relation to others, these activities are actually deemed to be less important, but mean values calculated are still close to agree. Furthermore, they fall into the group of less supported and less successfully performed KMAs, which additionally justifies their practical progression when focused on improving organisational learning and knowledge dissemination. At last, one must highlight that the portfolio comparison shows that activity *"9-restrict access and protect digital resources"*, though less supported than others, is still deemed to be one of the most successfully performed KMAs.

Summing up on the whole, the portfolios contrasting importance/success and support/success also brought closer the KMAs *"reflect on and refine work practices or processes"* and *"find people with particular knowledge or expertise"* as most interesting. Both are deemed to be important, whereas less supported and less successfully performed activities. Further, correlations between perceived support and perceived importance are stronger than correlations between perceived importance and perceived support, leading to the assumption that not everything organizations do to support a knowledge maturing activity (perceived support) is heading in the right direction (perceived importance). But what they do to support KMAs (perceived support), seems to aid performance (perceived success).

As given notice, interviewees were also appealed for suggesting new knowledge maturing activities. Mainly, the set of KMAs as found in the ethnographically-informed study and subjected to validation in the large scale interview study seem stable as there are only a few additions. Some showed mere refinements of the proposed KMAs, like product testing (which is covered by "rate, assess, and verify artefact") or organisational reflection, whereas the majority of novel activities (6 distinct activities, 10 in total) were related to a guidance perspective.

3.4 FURTHER READING

Kaschig, Andreas, Maier, Ronald, Sandow, Alexander, Lazoi, Mariangela, Barnes, Sally-Anne, Bimrose, Jenny, Bradley, Claire, Brown, Alan, Kunzmann, Christine, Mazarakis, Athanasios, Schmidt, Andreas (2010). Knowledge Maturing Activities and Practices Fostering Organisational Learning: Results of an Empirical Study. In: Sustaining TEL: From Innovation to Learning and Practice 5th European Conference on Technology Enhanced Learning, EC-TEL 2010, Barcelona, Spain, September 28 - October 1, 2010. Proceedings, Lecture Notes in Computer Science vol. 6383, Springer, 2010, pp. 151-166 http://publications.andreas.schmidt.name/ECTEL2010_KnowledgeMaturingActivities.pdf

Kaschig, A., Maier, R., Sandow, A. & Schmidt, A. (Eds.) (2010). D1.2 - Results Of The Representative Study And Refined Conceptual Knowledge Maturing Model. Deliverable of the FP7 IP MATURE, Section 4.5, http://d.mature-ip.eu/D1.2

4

Observing and Measuring Knowledge Maturing: Indicators and Scorecard

Knowledge Maturing Indicators make knowledge maturing traceable. They can be used for diagnosing, monitoring, and evaluating knowledge maturing.

4.1   CONCEPT

Knowledge maturing processes are hard to observe and measure, for example in terms of efficiency. Still, measurability is crucial for several aspects:

- The appropriate forms of learning and way of dealing with knowledge differs considerably between the maturing phases so that any tool supporting knowledge maturing needs to be aware of the maturity. This can only be achieved if indicators are at hand that can be calculated automatically and can be feed into the tools themselves.

- Incremental approaches with feedback are key to successfully introducing knowledge maturing. Based on indicators, effects of initiatives aiming at supportive knowledge maturing are made transparent and comprehensible.

- Measures to improve knowledge maturing need to be integrated with other forms of controlling to justify investments made and track their contribution towards overall business goals of the company.

These aspects are quite diverse and therefore require indicators at different levels of abstraction.

It has been found that it is difficult to come up with direct, context-free and universally applicable measures for knowledge maturing or knowledge maturity. By now, Knowledge Maturing Indicators (KMIs) have been conceived as observable events or states that need to be interpreted carefully. In order to support the evaluation of the construct knowledge maturing, which yet alone is difficult to measure, especially in combination one can only suggest that knowledge maturing has happened. It proves that knowledge maturing is a complex, multi-faceted phenomenon and is hardly directly observable. Direct measures have not been found yet to help assess whether and to what extent knowledge maturing has happened. However, finding at least indicators that help to assess knowledge maturing are important for two reasons which also reflect two very different levels of granularity that our KMI adhere to:

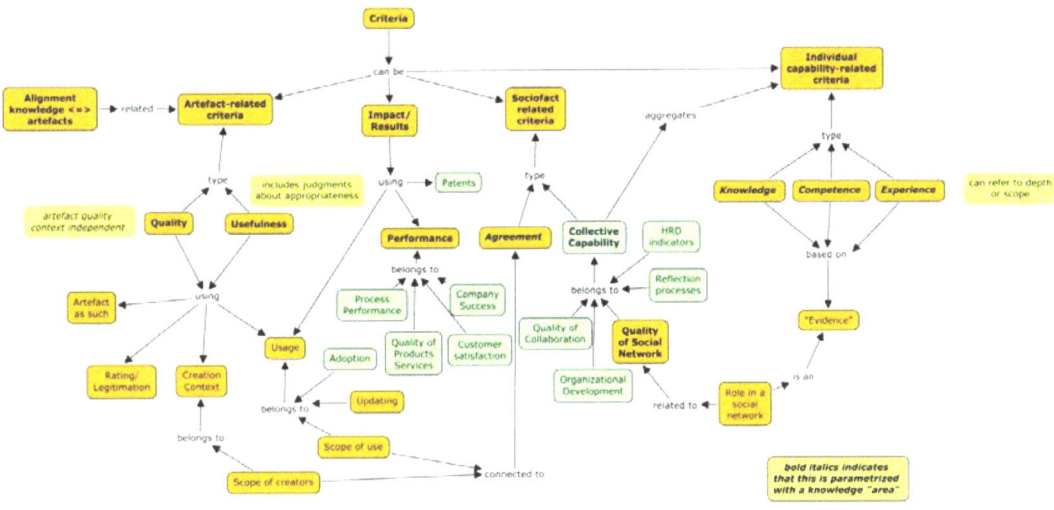

Figure 7. Context map of knowledge maturing indicators and related concepts

Management level

The management level is important as we envision the knowledge maturing concept as not only a merely descriptive concept, but one that individuals in organisations can act upon when deciding on how to guide or what measures to apply on or what tools to use to support goal-oriented learning on a collective level. The old management saying that "You can only manage what you can measure" resonates with many practitioners that were talked to in preparation of an empirical study. Frequent questions about how one should go about measuring that knowledge maturing has happened and which in turn would make it possible to trace the impact of interventions into improving knowledge maturing. The measures sought after at this level are coarse-granular, aggregated and value-oriented.

IT Service level

KMIs are also explored to be able to (semi-) automatically recognise matured organisational knowledge. Knowledge maturing indicators are highly relevant for maturing services to detect and support knowledge maturing. The vision of such IT services is to automatically analyse combined workspaces of knowledge workers and present results of the analysis in the form of one or a set of indicators. The measures sought after at this level are fine-granular, atomic and oriented towards the media and portion of the digital space that they analyse.

Within a multi-phase empirical study a list of KMIs was developed in a multi-step process: theoretically elaborated, reflected in context of what might be termed knowledge maturing events and validated in the large scale interview study, where the list was used as guideline to 139 interviews. The KMIs arose as a concept to support the assessment of (changes in) maturity of knowledge, as requirements to the design of possible maturing services and as a tool for evaluation.

As insights surfaced during the development of a comprehensive list of KMIs, the need for a systematic approach was unavoidable:

- As knowledge can be related to different media, KMIs were structured according to knowledge embedded in a digital resource, held by a person and embedded in processes. Combinations of these media types were investigated to depict possible KMIs, but for being too heterogeneous and for the double nature of process (both as a process model artefact and as a socio-fact) the approach led to difficulties in practice.

- Indicators are to be formulated as states or as state changes (e.g., an artefact has a certain degree of structuredness or has changed its degree of structuredness). Indicators could refer to a single event (e.g., an artefact has been changed), to a number of events within a time frame (e.g., an artefact has been changed frequently in the last 7 days), or even a change in frequency within a time frame compared to previous time frames (e.g., an artefact has been changed more frequently within the last 7 days than in the weeks before). The higher order derivation with respect to states and events variants, although blurry to real-world settings, is important for formulation and interpretation of indicators. Focus is on the fact that with an event something occurred in a specific instant in time, while for the state perspective results are looked at.

- Indicators can be aggregated or combined for more complex, derived indicators to yield a higher semantic expressivity (through a more concrete understanding of the actual activity), e.g. event sequences like "an artefact has been changed after an individual has attended training". Such a concept has a number of attributes and properties deemed to be appropriate for describing the state of KM.

- Contextualizing indicators has patterns of variants emerge where a common structural composition is observable based upon a subject (manifestation of knowledge), a base form (conceptual core, e.g. "change", "legitimate", "be involved"), a variant (generation of actual state of maturity) and context conditions (restrictions set upon variants such as specified time frames for changes, mandatory use of existing or aggregated indicators and an intended purpose to reach).

- Similar but semantically different variants of indicators can be created leading to combinatorial explosion or they seem arbitrary (when selecting some of the possible variants), while other context conditions (e.g., specific types of artefact, qualities of individuals etc.) can be used to narrow down a specific knowledge maturing indicator like a drill-down in data analysis.

Amalgamating the deepened understanding driven from the several considerable aspects above, a classification hierarchy was approached with profound distinctions and even providing a basis to define a more abstract, intermediate layer between knowledge maturing and the indicators.

Classification of Indicators

The guiding principle for the top level classification is a clear statement to what is actually being made traceable, about what a statement is to make or which manifestation of knowledge exists. This has led to the distinctions *artefact (digital resources)*, and *socio fact (persons)*, while cognifact (processes) was split into *individual capabilities* and *topic* (where topics were directly observed). In the large-scale interview study, we tested a number of indicators. The analysis according to these dimensions led to the conclusion that process-related KMIs were deemed the most suitable for measuring knowledge maturing in organisations, whereas digital-resource related KMIs were deemed less suitable.

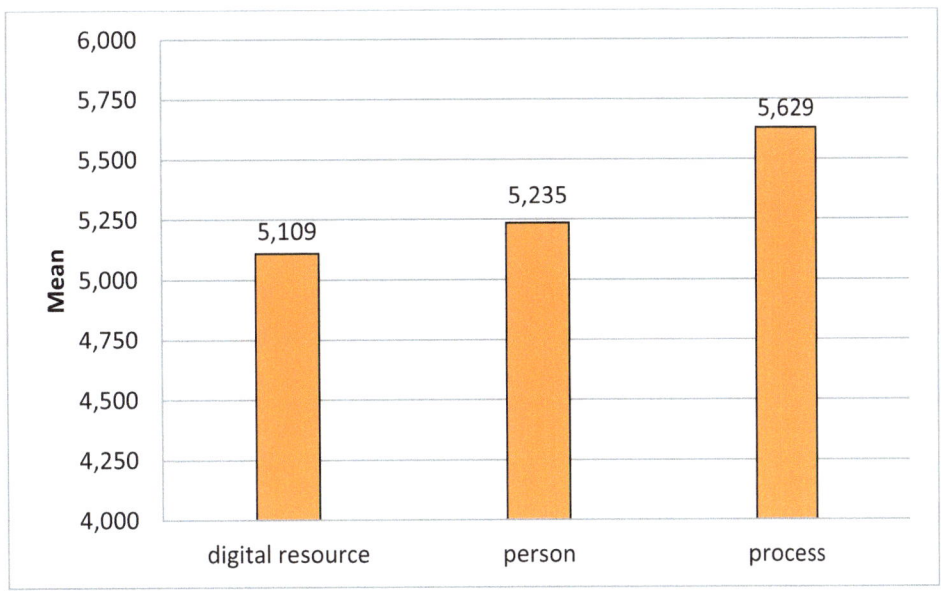

Figure 8. Mean values per dimension of KMIs

Additionally, an output-oriented category *impact/performance* was included (see Figure 9). On the second level (and third level where necessary) a conceptual approach is to explain how the aspects, intended to make traceable, are related to knowledge maturing. In some case, deviations from this general approach had mere groupings introduced (e.g., "individual - organization", "individual – group").

Indicator category "Impact and Performance" differs from the other indicator categories as they are general indicators not specific to knowledge maturing, but found in many other indicator systems. As from business perspective, knowledge maturing is a means, an instrument, applied in order to achieve results that comprise a business value in a narrow sense. Therefore, analysis in more detail should lead to how KMI fit into other organizational indicator systems. KMIs refer to the process of handling knowledge in organizations within core and service business processes rather than to inputs or outputs of these processes. Consequently, a tool for monitoring knowledge management initiatives can also be integrated with existing controlling tools used in an organization to increase visibility of KM initiatives and to link to organisational inputs and goals.

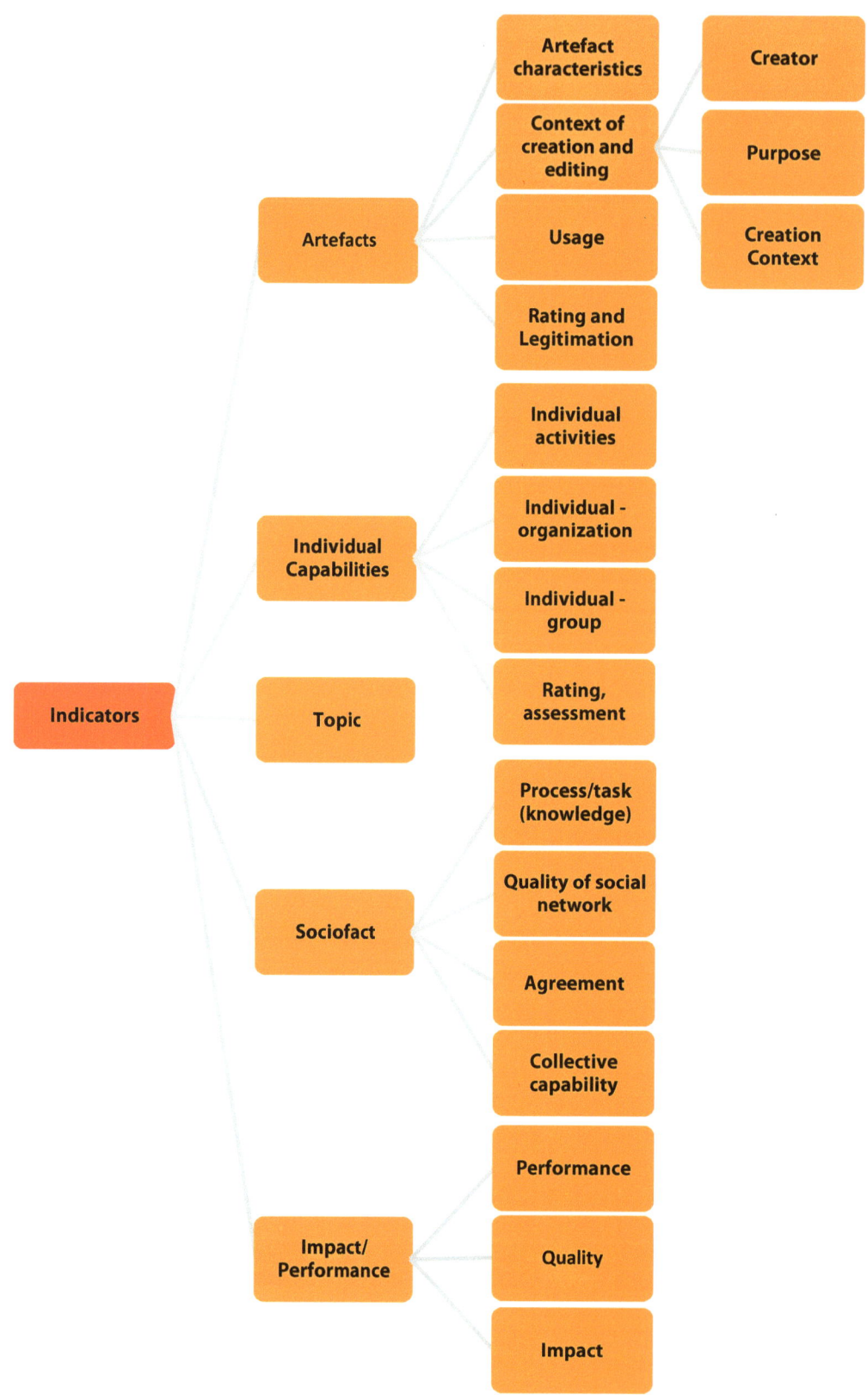

Figure 9. Structure of Knowledge Maturing Indicators

Finally, as given notice, further aim was pointed at defining an intermediate layer between knowledge maturing and the indicators and explanatory connections between them. The main criteria are shortly identified, reflecting on elaborated concepts of defining knowledge as cognifacts, socio-facts and artefacts, detailed results are presented in section 4.3:

- **Artefact-related** comprising indicators which measure aspects related to any form of artefact (corresponding to the dimension of the same name).

- **Individual capability-related** comprising indicators on the individual's experience, competence, or knowledge.

- **Socio-fact-related** covering indicators measuring quality of social interaction or meta-competencies on a collective level.

- **Alignment of artefacts and cognifacts.** Resulted from analysing the demonstrators which all aim at aligning the maturity or formality of artefacts with the maturity of the underlying knowledge, avoiding over- and under-formalization.

- **Impact & Results.** One of the major additions led by interviewees that indirectly measures maturity of knowledge through the output it generates. However, these are also most context-specific, i.e. they need to take into account the goals of the business system, business processes as well as complementary initiatives, such as quality management initiatives.

4.2   IN-DEPTH CONSIDERATIONS AND SCIENTIFIC CONTEXT

As pointed out above, this section is thought to deepen the understanding on findings of an intermediate layer between knowledge maturing and the framed hierarchy to classified indicators. Explanatory connections are to ease the deployment of indicators by selecting after whichever criteria one assesses knowledge maturing initiatives.

4.2.1   Artefact related criteria

Artefact related criteria seem to be the most straightforward criteria to use because artefacts (if they are in a digital form) are easy to access and analyse. But what can be derived from characteristics of artefacts about the collective knowledge in an organisation that they supposedly help to materialise?

The underlying *assumptions* are the following:

- A higher quality (fitness for use or usefulness) of artefacts reflects the maturity of the underlying knowledge. One cannot produce a high-quality artefact without having sufficiently mature knowledge.

- Because knowledge maturing expands the scope of the "audience" of that knowledge, this usually involves boundary crossing for which appropriate artefacts are produced as boundary objects so that one can also assume that artefacts will be produced. However, this is also a limitation: this criterion can only cover knowledge that can be and is made explicit.

- A different perspective is a more collective one that does not aim at an individual piece of knowledge, but rather at an organizational capacity: if the organization is able to produce high-quality artefacts, it also has effective knowledge maturing processes (underlying assumption that high process quality leads to high product or service quality).

For artefact-related criteria, we have identified two sub criteria:

- **Quality.** This refers to characteristics that are inherent to the artefacts or at least not dependent on a context, e.g., the customer context. This includes indicators for the artefacts as such, e.g. readability, link density, structuredness, etc.

- **Usefulness.** Quality does not mean that it is useful for someone if quality is not defined with respect to fitness for use or from a customer perspective, but as conformance to requirements from a producer perspective. High quality artefacts in that latter sense can be useless, while low quality artefacts can be helpful sometimes. This sub criterion therefore includes judgments about appropriateness.

Both sub-criteria can utilize the same kind of indicators, but with different interpretation (and potentially slightly different settings) or rating/assessment: you can assess a document with respect to quality from a context-free producer perspective, from an application perspective taking into account the context of creation. Meaning, you can assess it according to how useful it was for your own problem situation in which you have used it, or taking into account the context of potential re-use, i.e. reflecting the customer perspective. Likewise, you can interpret usage indicators in terms of usefulness or quality. If it gets updated, it could be traced back to its low quality or to its usefulness, which makes it worth updating. Further criteria related to quality or usefulness derives information from the creation context: "who created it, how diverse was the group, for which purpose was it created?" and from the context of reuse: "who might reuse it, how diverse might that group be, for which purpose might it be reused?"

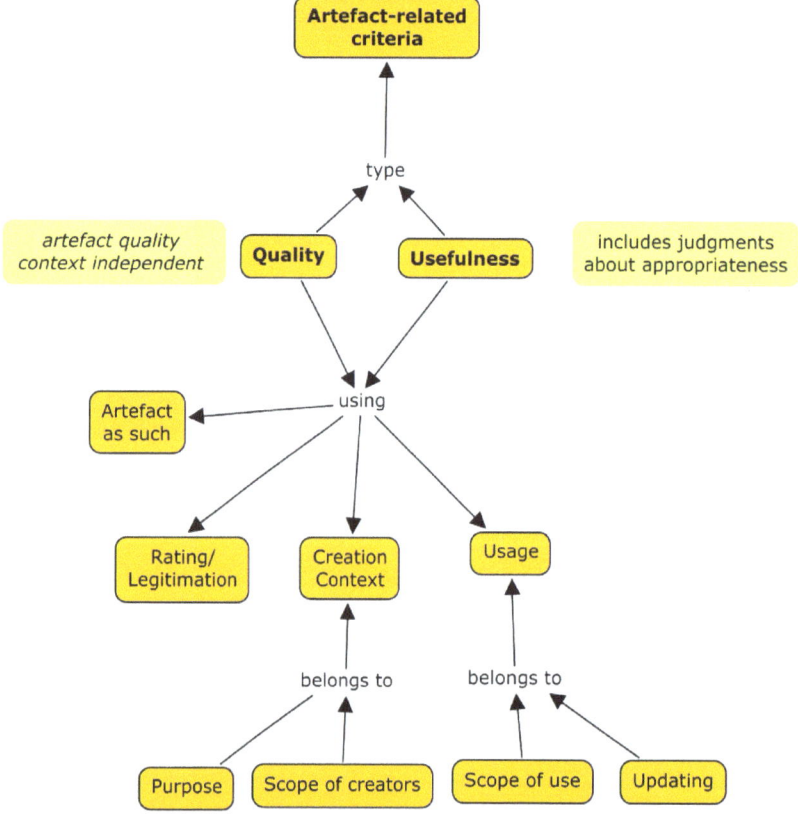

Figure 10. Artefact-related criteria

4.2.2 *Individual capability-related*

This criterion covers the contribution of individual learning to knowledge maturing. We have distinguished knowledge maturing from individual learning, where the former is an advancement of knowledge on the collective level while the latter is limited to advancements on the individual level. Individual learning, therefore, is a prerequisite for knowledge maturing, but not sufficient (see section 2).

However, interviewees frequently had concerns and brought forward that experience can also have an opposite effect on knowledge maturing as it makes you professionally blinkered (skilled incompetence). Meaning, one cannot simply take a cumulative perspective (i.e., the amount/duration of experience), but that the diversity of experiences needs to be taken into account. In some cases even, employees coming from outside are seen as one of the major triggers for knowledge maturing, sometimes much more than internal sources.

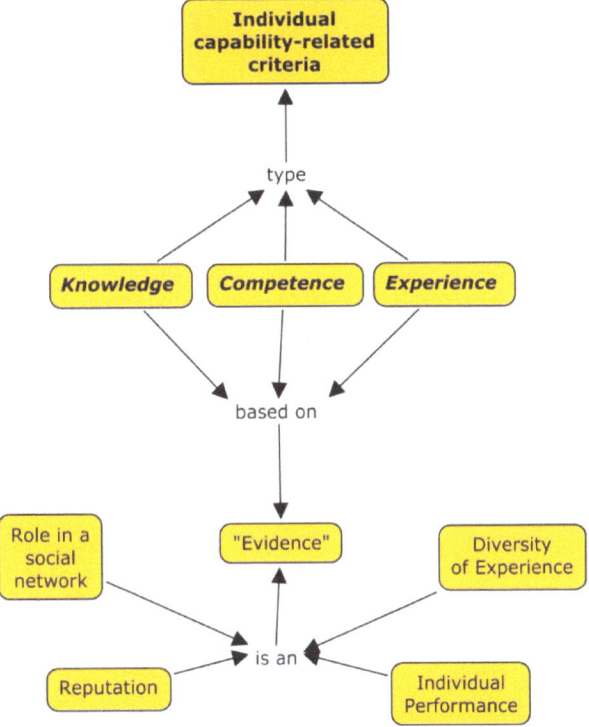

Figure 11. Individual Capability-Related Criteria

Even if arguing that individual capability is a good criterion for knowledge maturing, it remains a hard problem to assess. That again is well-known to areas of competence management (competence diagnosis) and also to emerging domains of e-portfolios and certification of informal learning outcomes, where one speaks of "evidence" for a certain competency or experience. It remains a challenging task because competence, knowledge, experience, is frequently as unobservable as knowledge maturing is. Further, it is of no big use to consider "experience" or "competence" of an individual in general, because they are always related to certain competency domains or areas of experience. As so with "evidence", which is highly contextualized and its inseparable context from a more general competency makes it as methodologically challenging.

4.2.3 Socio-fact-related

Socio-facts which comprise rules, collective practices etc. are much less accessible for assessment than the artefact-related criteria. Still, socio-facts represent an important source for learning about knowledge maturing.

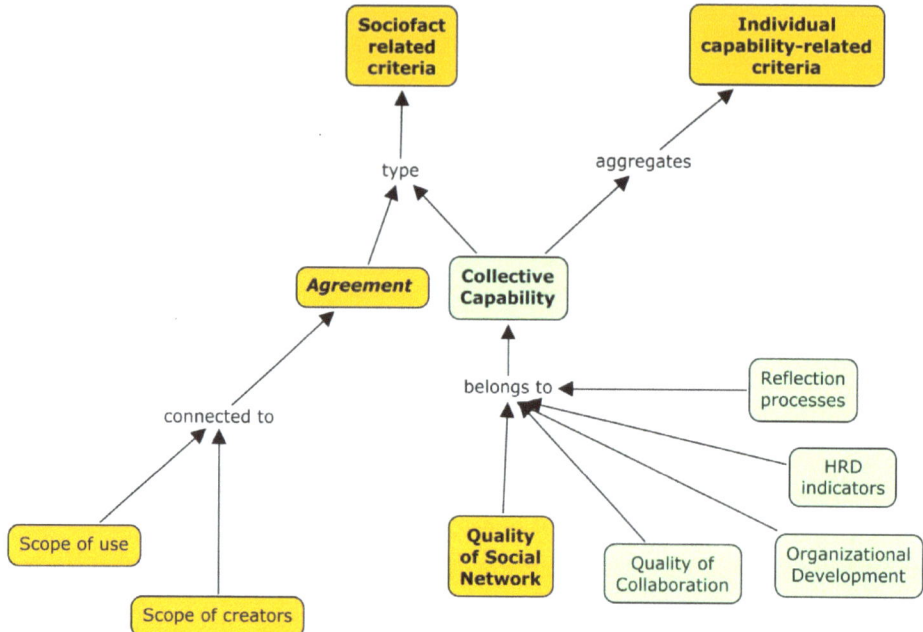

Figure 12: Sociofact-related Criteria

- On a more specific level, it is assumed that the more mature knowledge is to a subject, the higher the level of agreement is in the collective. This is most obvious if it is about ontological knowledge, i.e. knowledge how to describe things. A shared vocabulary can only be mature if it is really shared and agreed upon by the respective group. But this can also be illustrated for process knowledge, where an expert designs a process still being immature and only becoming so if the process becomes part of daily practice, contributing the knowledge to operationalize it. An overlap with artefact-related criteria is denoted like the scope of use or scope of creators which indicate a degree of agreement. On a more collective level, it is assumed that organizational competencies to learn are a prerequisite for mastering knowledge maturing processes. A learning organization is more capable of knowledge maturing. Again, this perspective was largely introduced through the interviews, where a lot of indicators around human resources development, quality of collaboration, the presence of reflective processes, or even the fact that the organisation develops further were mentioned. This can be viewed as a collective capability, which aggregates individual capabilities.

4.2.4   Impact & Results

The impact-related criteria follow the philosophy of typical KPI systems (key performance indicators) in companies where the focus is on what criteria are measurable and have a clear relationship to organizational goals. This set of criteria thus materialises an important connection between knowledge maturing and the (operational) management, reporting and controlling system of an organisation. Organisations are not interested in capability as such, but in the success of applying it in a concrete business process, activity or market situation. The assumptions behind it are the following:

- If knowledge how to produce, organise or consult is mature, then the results are better than with immature knowledge, following the perspective that knowledge is a resource or production factor. Building collective knowledge, thus, is capacity building for the organisation. But this also implies that the value of knowledge is connected to a purpose, clearly the differentiation between "pure" knowledge and "relevant" knowledge.

- Efficient processes must be well understood and agreed upon with the stakeholders, requiring mature process knowledge.

- On the collective level, assumedly the success of the organisation/team is connected to whether knowledge maturing takes place successfully, e.g. that the actual product or service reflects how the company deals with knowledge.

- A major limitation to this criterion is that it is a retrospective criterion by nature: it can only measure the impact/result of knowledge acquired in the past and cannot judge the future impact or future results. Indicators here have a clear bias towards supporting evolutionary development and sustaining innovation, and tend to undervalue revolutionary developments and disruptive innovation.

The fact that indicators related to this criterion are already part of everyday (management) practice in companies, it was for the empirical study to spot the formerly under-developed performance instruments for supplementing the set of indicators related to impact and results. One interviewed company even views their (performance) indicators as their major management instrument, including tracing RoI, but also as an incentive system for self-organised change processes in divisions and departments across a geographically distributed company network. Companies of physical goods see patents as easy to measure and as significant an indicator. Further included was the quality of products or services (including error rates, but also more soft issues like product identification), customer satisfaction, or the overall company success (e.g., in selling products or acquiring follow-up projects).

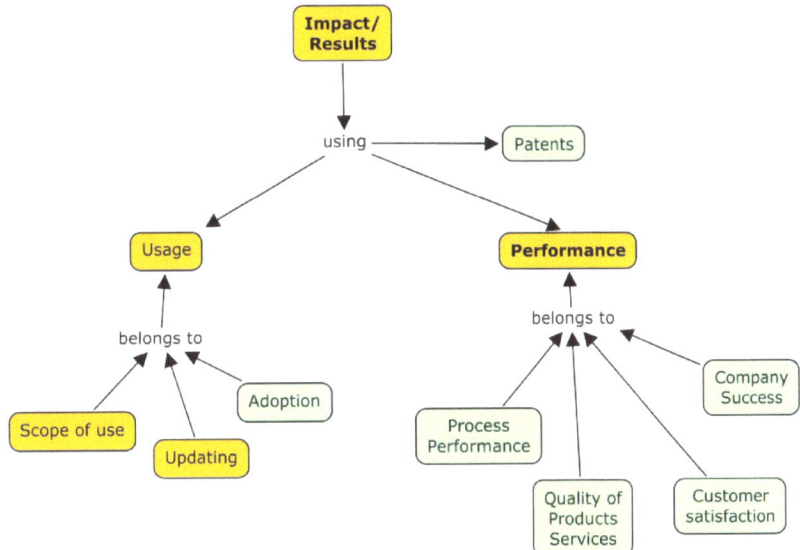

Figure 13. Impact-related Criteria

4.2.5   *Alignment of artefacts and cognifacts*

From the reflection on demonstrators by the ethnographical-informed study, one important additional aspect has emerged that did not easily fit into the other categories: the alignment of artefacts and cognifacts.

The underlying assumptions here are:

- Artefacts are required for effective knowledge maturing, especially in their function as boundary objects.

- Their format or level of formality has to be appropriate for the actual maturity of knowledge, avoiding over-formalisation and under-formalisation.

4.3 FURTHER READING

Kaschig, A., Maier, R., Sandow, A. & Schmidt, A. (Eds.) (2010). D1.2 - Results Of The Representative Study And Refined Conceptual Knowledge Maturing Model. Deliverable of the FP7 IP MATURE, Section 4.6, http://d.mature-ip.eu/D1.2

Kaschig, A., Maier, R., Sandow, A. & Schmidt, A. (Eds.) (2011). D1.3 Results of In-depth Case Studies, Recommendations and Final Knowledge Maturing Model. Deliverable of the FP7 IP MATURE, Section 4.5, http://d.mature-ip.eu/D1.3

Kunzmann, C., Schmidt. A. (Eds.) (2011), D9.2 Business Model for ASP. Deliverable of the FP7 IP MATURE, Section 4

5

Overcoming Barriers to Knowledge Maturing: Motivational and Cultural Aspects

Knowledge maturing depends on the engagement of individuals. Understanding motivational and factors and barriers is key to holistic knowledge maturing support. A model for analysing motivational and cultural barriers helps to identify an organization's problems and potential solutions.

5.1 CONCEPT

While it is generally acknowledged that motivational, social, and cultural aspects are crucial for changing workplace practice, it turns out to be difficult to include this aspect into design processes. MATURE has therefore (i) developed an analysis model that allows for systematic addressing of motivational aspects and (ii) conducted empirical studies on relevant barriers.

Based on an extension of the model for workplace behaviour by (Comelli and von Rosenstiel, 2003), the influencing factors on the engagement in a concrete knowledge maturing activity can be decomposed into three main aspects (figure 14):

- **Individual**. This aspect refers to factors that originate directly in the personality and personal characteristics of the individual. Two basic families of factors can be identified:
  - **Capability** describes factors that affect whether an individual can engage in knowledge maturing activities. This comprises cognitive abilities to understand the issues at hand, and meta competencies, e.g., to cooperate, or to explain to others.
  - **Interests, values and needs** affect whether an individual wants to engage in knowledge maturing activities. These interests can be rational goals, e.g., for one's own career, but also comprise personal values, e.g., personal quality standards, and needs, e.g., for appreciation.
- The **work context** consists of organisational prerequisites for engagement in knowledge maturing activities:
  - **Organisational** factors affect whether the individual is allowed to or is even supposed to engage in concrete maturing activities, i.e., it comprises authorization, legitimation, commitment, rewarding, among others.
  - **Enabling** factors refer to the technical and non-technical facilities offered or tolerated by the organisation to engage in knowledge maturing activities. This comprises technical systems like document and knowledge management systems, email, instant messaging, but also coffee machines and water coolers as

possibilities for social interaction. Frequently, not only the facilities as such, but also the implicit and explicit regulations for their usage form an important part.

- The **interpersonal context** is equally important as most knowledge maturing activities involve interpersonal communication and cooperation.

  o **Cooperative** factors refer to cooperation as such and its inherent conflicts of interest from a more rational point of view. As cooperation in a single activity is frequently asymmetric, mismatches of interest occur so that win-win situations do not form.

  o **Affective** factors refer to the emotional side of social relationships and how the involved individual views the quality of these relationships. This includes factors like trust, or "personal chemistry".

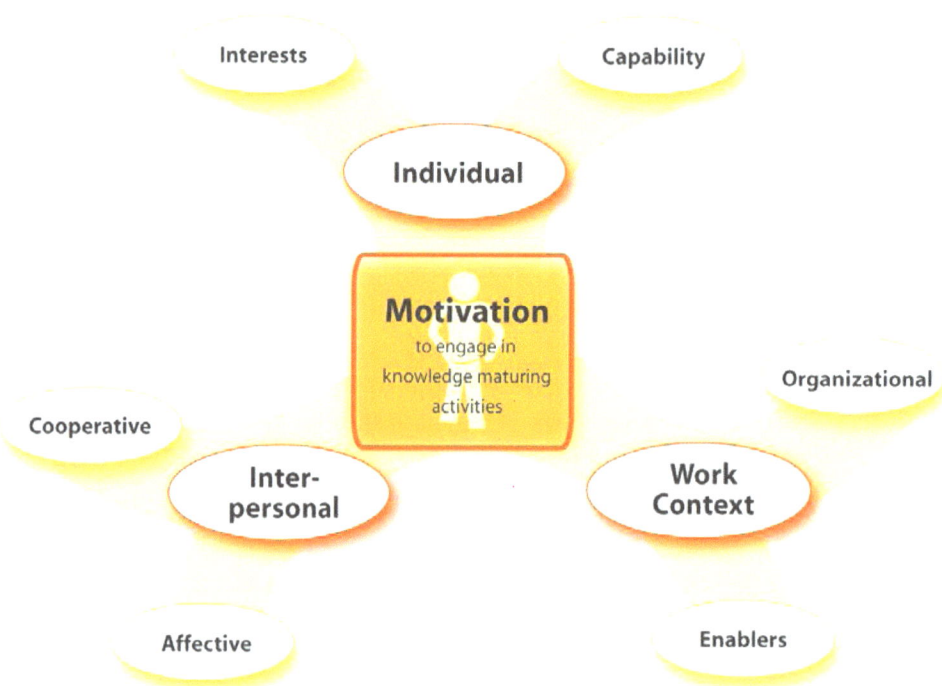

Figure 14: Determinants of motivation to engage in knowledge maturing activities

These factors cannot be clearly separated and also have at least long-term interdependencies:

- Capabilities of the individual can be improved by organisational measures (giving more responsibilities). This in turn can result in a shift of interest as self-esteem has risen. A change in interest changes the fundamentals of cooperation.

- The organisation can also introduce technologies that promote transparency and participation. This can conflict with or transform the corporate culture which in turn influences the foundations of cooperation, e.g., changes the value of competition vs. cooperation.

In section 5.3, we investigate each of these aspects in more detail with respect to:

- identifying the set of individual factors (non-exhaustive) and ways to understand them,

- identifying the barriers related to those factors,

- and potential interventions to overcome these barriers.

5.2   PRACTICAL RELEVANCE

The model allows for a systematic approach to motivational barriers and separates different aspects. But how to move on from here towards a systematic integration into the design process? One important lesson of the MATURE project was that it was highly beneficial to have software developers as (a part of) the ethnographers. While the original purpose of the ethnographic studies has been in the first run primarily to inform the concept development, it has turned out that taking part in those studies, i.e., immersing into a team of people at their workplaces, creates a very deep understanding of problems, needs, barriers etc. (in short: the target users' reality). This has created a fundamentally different level of shared understanding between technical developers and application partners.

Based on those experiences, we propose the following methodology, which is evaluated as part of current project activities:

- **Immersion of technical developers in the workplace reality** as part of rapid ethnographically informed studies with a focus on motivational aspects and guided by the model as presented in the previous section

- **Derivation of personas**, i.e. a precise description of a user's characteristics and what he/she wants to accomplish [Cooper 99] as a real world person with an explicit consideration of the three aspects of the model (i.e., what is the individual/interpersonal/organizational context of the persona that influences her motivational structure)

- **Development of use case descriptions** for those personas in direct interaction of developments and users (or their representatives), with an explicit section on interventions targeted to motivational aspects or context conditions

- **Deriving functional and non-functional requirements** from those descriptions

- **Formative evaluation of early prototypes** with end users in which – if possible – different motivational measures are compared to each other in order select the most effective one.

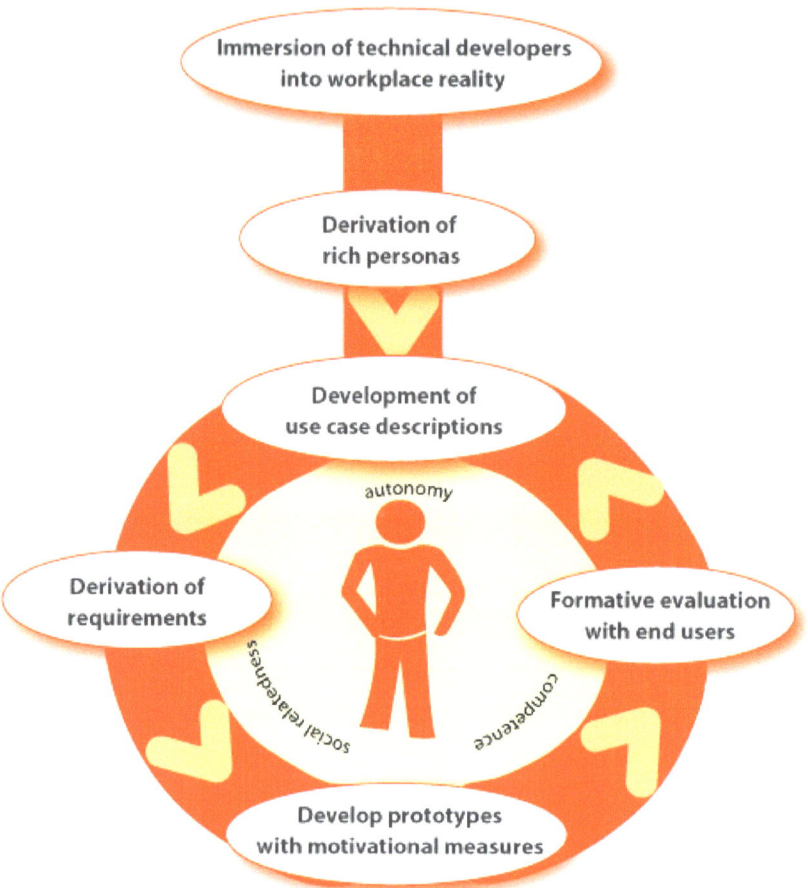

Figure 15: Integrating motivational aspects into the design process

As an illustration of the role of persona descriptions, here is an excerpt of a persona description that includes motivational aspects:

"Silke has high personal standards and aims at continuously learning to improve her work practice. To that end, she regularly reflects about how tasks were carried out and what could have been done better or worse. Based on those insights, she updates templates and process descriptions. Where possible, she discusses her experiences with others. She also regularly visits the operational departments in order to learn about the current situation, problems, and developments. She has very high personal standards and is committed to improving her work practice in all aspects. She is very open and interested, also in topic not directly related to her current work situation. She tries to make sense of new trends. Her sense of perfection also applies to her everyday task management. She plans her tasks and appointment each day meticulously, and prepares each meeting with elaborate notes. She always uses paper and pencil for that, and she needs the feeling of satisfaction of ticking off completed items. She often has problems with the usability of computer software. Particularly, labels, buttons, and icons should be uniform across different applications and should not change with software updates. Clear structures within the applications are crucial as she lacks deep knowledge about computers."

5.3   IN-DEPTH CONSIDERATIONS AND SCIENTIFIC CONTEXT

Psychology has brought forth plenty of different models trying to conceptualize behavioural structures of **interests, values, and needs** of individuals:

- Maslow (1954) structures the needs into different layers and introduces dependencies between them in the form of a hierarchy: physiological, safety, love/belonging, esteem, and self-actualization.

- Herzberg et al. (1959) distinguish between different motivational factors: motivators and hygiene factors. While the latter form prerequisites for satisfaction (and can only have a negative effect if not fulfilled), the first ones cause positive effects on intrinsic motivation.

- Deci & Ryan (2000) identify three basic needs for intrinsic motivation:

  - experiencing autonomy,

  - experiencing competence,

  - experiencing relatedness.

- Values are the result of socialization processes which are developed in a life-long process. Value systems can be influenced through the social context (including the organisational context).

As the knowledge maturing model suggests with the level of meta-competencies, individuals need certain **capabilities** to engage in knowledge maturing activities. If these capabilities are missing, barriers arise. Some of these barriers are specific to the situation; others arise in most cases that could lead to knowledge maturing. In the latter cases, this can practically prevent individuals from participating in knowledge maturing in general.

- The individuals cannot express their ideas or understanding. This could be traced back to the fact that it is already sufficiently developed, but the individuals lack the competency to express themselves. Another reason could be that the expression as such still needs a learning process (i.e., the knowledge is not mature enough). This particularly applies to procedural knowledge, in contrast to declarative knowledge.

- Communication processes as such have inherent difficulties, which could hamper efficient exchange. The gap between communicating partners could lack a common ground.

5.3.1   *Factors and Barriers on the Interpersonal Level*

Cooperation within organisations is a sensitive topic. While on a global scale, cooperation is essential and beneficial, on the individual level these immediate benefits are not equally distributed within a single activity, sometimes not even on a longer time scale. Such asymmetries are analyzed within various contexts:

Game theory explores cooperation behaviour of actors under uncertainty about the behaviour of the other. The prisoners' dilemma provides a classical example that on a global scale, cooperative behaviour is preferable, but for each individual with a local perspective, non-cooperation seems to be the better choice. In Figure 16, if both players 1 and 2 share their knowledge, each of them will have a benefit of 7. But if player 1 cooperates, but player 2 does not, player 1 will only have a benefit of 3 and player 2 will have 9. In purely rational behaviour, this will mean that player 1 and 2 will decide not to share.

player 1	player 2		
	strategy	share knowledge	defection

	share knowledge	A (7/7)	B (3/9)
	Defection	C (9/3)	D (5/5)

Figure 16: Prisoners' dilemma

As a consequence, we can already identify that (1) expectancy of reciprocity and (2) immediate benefits for the individual are important factors.

Furthermore, we need to consider the issue of power which has been a major barrier when implementing knowledge management instruments in companies. The power-dependency theory of Emerson[2] helps to understand an activity of knowledge sharing in terms of power. The theory explains that in exchange relationships where partner A needs the good partner B possesses, B can exercise power over A. In terms of knowledge: if B has the knowledge A needs, B can exercise power on A. Sharing the knowledge with B would result in a **loss of power**.

Beyond one-to-one relationships, the issue of the social dilemma has been analyzed for collaboration systems like wikis, forums or similar. Here, the decision situation whether to engage by contributing or whether to just make use of the available information ("free riding") is more complex. Experimental findings[3] suggest that

- lowering contribution costs
- making transparent the benefits to others
- and the identifiability of one's own contributions

significantly enhance the sharing behaviour.

Rather than emphasizing the "natural barriers" to cooperation, the research strand on "cooperative intelligence" views this as a competence development topic of individuals and collectives (e.g., organizations).[4]

Affective factors are frequently ignored as they represent unwanted human behaviour within organisations. Also, emotions between individuals (as their origin is highly contextual) can hardly be addressed on a general level. Still the ethnographic studies have shown that they constitute very frequent barriers in organizations.

5.3.2 Factors and Barriers on the Work Context Level

Burke & Litwin (1992) have systematized causal relationships for change processes in **organisations** which can also serve for identifying the influencing factors.

For the engagement in knowledge maturing activities, the most important factors are:

- **Organisational culture** is a pattern of shared assumptions which have been learnt and have proven useful while coping with internal and external conflicts and is thus binding (Schein, 1995). It represents the social framework for acceptable and desired behaviour in a

---

[2]   Emerson, R.: Power-Dependence Relations. American Sociological Review, Vol. 27, No. 1. (1962), pp. 31-41.

[3]   Riss, U., Cress, U., Kimmerle, J., & Martin, S. (2006). Knowledge transfer by sharing task patterns: From experiment to application. In J. S. Edwards (Ed.), Proceedings of KMAC2006, The Third Knowledge Management Aston Conference (pp. 121-133). Birmingham: Operational Research Society

[4]   Kauke, M.: Kooperative Intelligenz: Sozialpsychologische und spielexperimentelle Grundlagen der Interaktivität zwischen Partnern.Spektrum, Akad. Verl., 1998

company. Such a culture is constituted by unwritten rules, shared values, and a feeling of identity. Important aspects of such a corporate culture for the engagement in knowledge maturing activities are:

- o **Communication culture.** Communication lies at the heart of many cultural issues in organisations. Communication is the vehicle for leadership, it can implement transparency and enable participation.

- o **Culture of trust.** As we have seen on the cooperative level, trust can overcome barriers introduced by short-term advantages for non-cooperation and can lower the uncertainty about the behaviour of others which has an impact on the social dilemma. A corporate culture which is based on a positive mindset about the nature of employees will rely on openness and transparency instead of control. As a result, individuals within such an organisation will tend to assume reciprocity, and the importance of power diminishes for the attainment of personal goals.

- o **Culture of innovation.** This covers the valuing of new ideas, the challenging of dominant opinions and established procedures.

For influencing the corporate culture towards overcoming barriers to knowledge maturing, (Mayeroff and Gaylin, cited from von Krogh, 1998) recommend to reinforce the following five dimensions (which have an impact on the interpersonal level as well):

- • *mutual trust*: Trust compensates for lack of knowledge about other people and is necessary in order to ensure that people can help each other – to give and to accept help.

- • *active empathy*: Empathy means that a person can understand another person's situation, interests, skill level, history, opportunities and problems, "active" describes the situation when a person proactively seeks to understand another person.

- • *access to help*: Having access to help means that a person needing help is able to find it directly.

- • *leniency in judgment*: This dimension of care is especially needed when members of the organisation experiment with new solutions and produce errors; leniency means that these errors are not judged harshly which would possibly prevent future experimentation.

- • *courage*: Courage means that members of the organisation voice their opinions and give (real) feedback as part of a process to help each other.

- • **Organisational structure** can promote or prevent knowledge flow to happen. Next to informal organisational structures, deep hierarchies and fine-grained organisational divisions affect the maturing activities (Seidel 2003; Rosenstiel 2003):[5]

  - o *Compulsory coordination* with superior institution increases the costs of non-standard activities and cooperation across structural entities.

  - o *Centralisation and restricted information* channels allow for efficient coordination of a large organisation in the short run, but discourage self-initiated activities and thus also reduce the freedom of action.

- • **Corporate rules and regulations** limit the freedom of action for the actors in the organisation, thus reducing the experience of autonomy.

---

[5] Seidel, M.: Die Bereitschaft zur Wissensteilung; Wiesbaden 2003; Rosenstiel, L.: Führung durch Motivation, Wiesbaden 2003

- **Management practices** are important, for informal feedback on behaviour. Appreciation of maturing-relevant behaviour can foster the motivation of the individual.

Knowledge maturing activities in many cases can only occur if appropriate technical infrastructure **enables** them, i.e. allows for performing knowledge maturing activities. Based on Riege (2005) and the observations within the ethnographic studies, barriers in this area include

- low usability,

- mismatch between individuals' requirements and integrated IT systems and processes,

- low integration of IT systems,

- lack of compatibility between diverse IT systems and processes,

- lack of training regarding employee familiarisation with new IT systems and processes,

- lack of communication and demonstration of all advantages of any new system over existing ones,

- lack of technical support (internal and external) and immediate maintenance of integrated IT systems,

- lack of transparency and control.

5.3.3   Barriers and Knowledge Maturing Phases

Phase	Context	Issues to consider (e.g., motives or barriers to overcome)
I	*Individual*	<ul><li>need for experiencing autonomy</li><li>personal interest, curiosity</li><li>openness to learn and try out new things</li><li>satisfaction from achievments</li><li>resistance to change</li></ul>
	Cooperative	-
	Work	<ul><li>culture, valuing of creativity and new ideas</li><li>workload</li><li>lack of tools promoting reflection, creativity support, appropriation support and their usability</li></ul>
II	*Individual*	<ul><li>need for experiencing relatedness</li><li>lack of collaboration competencies</li><li>fear of openness</li><li>resistance to change</li></ul>
	Cooperative	<ul><li>economies of cooperation</li><li>social dynamics (reputation etc.)</li><li>team culture</li><li>tools promoting sharing, communication and their usability</li><li>reliability of shared spaces</li></ul>

	Work	<ul><li>complex regulations, e.g., for communicating with externals</li><li>tools for collaboration support</li><li>lack of cooperation infrastructure across boundaries</li><li>organizational fear of uncontrolled bottom-up activities</li><li>competitive situation => exchange with externals not wanted</li></ul>
III	Individual	<ul><li>experiencing competence</li><li>attribution of contributions and willingness to disseminate</li><li>personal sense of perfectionism</li></ul>
	Cooperative	<ul><li>affective barriers to accepting new approaches because of disliking the promoter</li><li>resistance to change</li></ul>
	Work	<ul><li>workload</li><li>lack of participation in decision processes</li><li>tools for searching and accessing existing artefacts</li><li>superiors not open to putting new knowledge to practice</li><li>reliability of shared spaces</li><li>frustration because of not relevant results when using shared spaces</li><li>lack of influence on shared spaces</li><li>media disruptions requiring additional efforts</li></ul>

IV	*Individual*	• personal sense of perfectionism • resistance to change
	Cooperative	• affective barriers to accepting new approaches because of disliking the promoter
	Work	• superiors not open to putting new knowledge to practice
V	*Individual*	• conflict with experiencing autonomy • reluctance to towards change (late adopters) • resistance to change
	Cooperative	
	Work	• lack of commitment to roll-out from executives • lack of resources • managerial practice

5.4 FURTHER READING

Kaschig, A., Maier, R., Sandow, A., Schmidt, A., Thalmann, S. (Eds.): D1.1 Results of the Ethnographic Study and Conceptual Knowledge Maturing Model, Deliverable 1.1 of the FP7 IP MATURE, Section 5.3 (pp. 61-70), http://d.mature-ip.eu/D1.1

> *Conceptualizations of motivational aspects in literature, integration into the motivational aspects analysis model, and linking of barriers and ways to overcome those barriers to the knowledge maturing phase model.*

Kaschig, A., Maier, R., Sandow, A., D1.2 Results of the Representative Study and Refined Conceptual Knowledge Maturing Model, Deliverable of the FP7 IP MATURE, Section 4.4.3 (pp. 52-58), http://d.mature-ip.eu/D1.2

> *Empirical results from a large-scale interview study on barriers in the different phases of the knowledge maturing process*

Kunzmann, Christine, Schmidt, Andreas, Braun, Volker, Czech, David, Fletschinger, Benjamin, Kohler, Silke, Lüber, Verena: Integrating Motivational Aspects into the Design of Informal Learning Support in Organizations. In: 9th International Conference on Knowledge Management and Knowledge Technologies, September 2-4, 2009, Graz, Austria, 2009, pp. 259-267

> *Motivational analysis model and embedding of motivational aspects into the design process*

6

Influencing Knowledge Maturing: The Concept of Guidance

Knowledge maturing processes can be improved through guidance. Guidance is any external influence on the direction or the quality of knowledge maturing processes. Both humans and tool can guide through guidance activities. These guidance activities offer a wide range of instruments for intervention.

Knowledge maturing does not only take place via bottom-up activities, driven by individual interests. It is equally important that these grassroot activities converge towards shared goals. This is particularly important for the later phases so that knowledge can have a larger impact and scope. How can we influence knowledge maturing processes? This leads us to the concept of guidance.

6.1   CONCEPT

Guidance in the context of knowledge maturing is any influence on the direction ("goal") or the quality (in terms of effectiveness and efficiency) of knowledge maturing processes by entities not directly involved in them. This definition of guidance neither specifies that this influence is intentional nor that it has positive effects on knowledge maturing because it is often difficult to judge (especially in advance) whether it has positive or negative effects.

Guidance is also not limited to persons as the "guiding" entity (like, e.g., leadership with respect to knowledge maturing), but is also exercised by artefacts (like documents containing guidelines), or sociofacts (like social rules, or a shared understanding). In the following, we have a closer look at these different forms of guidance.

6.1.1   Artefact-based Guidance

Artefacts such as reports, process models, guidelines, have an important function in knowledge maturing processes; they facilitate exchange and cooperation, and promote boundary crossing between different communities. This function has so far been mainly seen as artefacts being part of knowledge maturing processes by documenting their (intermediate) results. However, this is only one part of their role in knowledge maturing processes. They also guide other knowledge maturing processes in which they are not the object of development. The existence of a process model, even if it is not lived by, will influence future reflection on practice and the maturing of knowledge how to do certain things. Either the artefact is taken as a starting point which is improved, or the model is completely opposed and argued against it. But the development is not free from influence.

There is definitely a positive effect of artefact-based guidance: existing artefacts provide scaffolding; new developments can be compared to established artefacts, so this is important for the Zone of Proximal Development. The risk of artefact-based guidance lies in the constraints they impose on new ideas and developments. They tend to foster continuous evolution and sedimentation instead of revolutionary developments.

Not all artefacts have the same degree of influence on future knowledge maturing processes. The degree of influence of artefacts depends on many factors, which include:

- **Awareness of existence**. The existence of an artefact only affects knowledge maturing processes if the actors are aware of it. A filed guideline nobody knows about hardly can have any influence, whereas the same guideline will have an impact on the way of thinking if everyone is aware of it.

- **Legitimation**. Even if the content of a document is the same, it makes a difference whether it is an official document endorsed by top management or just authored by an employee. In the first case, it is more authoritative, thus considered more important. In the second case, it has to convince by its usefulness. The same applies also to persons as authorities for certain topics through their reputation.

- **Commitment.** The guiding influence of an artefact also depends on the amount of support it gets. In addition to legitimation, support can also be provided in the form of self-commitment by members of groups, teams, communities or other organizational units, i.e. the amount of identification of these entities with the knowledge materialised in the artefact.

- **Quality and usefulness**. Besides organisational legitimation, commitment or personal reputation, there is also inherent reputation of an artefact that originates from its quality and usefulness/appropriateness which in turn usually correlates with the maturity of knowledge it represents: more mature knowledge guides the development of new knowledge which – in a Kuhnian perspective – can lead to both stabilizing, but also revolutionary effects.

- **Level of formality**. The level of formality (or degree of structuredness) plays a big role for artefact-related guidance. Higher level of formality on the one hand constrains the freedom of action by eliminating ambiguity; on the other hand it helps to gain efficiency. This applies to all forms of artefacts: highly structured documents vs. informal notes, formal process models vs. task notes, formal ontologies vs. informal tags. This also applies on a meta-level: the formalism chosen/prescribed/recommended for a knowledge maturing activity influences the progress so that it is important to consider the appropriateness.

6.1.2 Sociofact-based Guidance

Not only artefacts, but also sociofacts (such as social rules, norms, or shared practice) influence knowledge maturing processes as knowledge maturing is a social learning process. The challenge with sociofacts is that they are usually much less visible, but their guidance effect can be much more intense. Based on the work so far, we can identify the following most important types of sociofacts that have a guiding effect:

- **Culture.** Culture includes shared values and unwritten rules about socially acceptable behaviour. It influences whether sharing is good, whether new ideas are welcome, how open organisational members are to externals etc. This implies that companies assumedly have different strengths in terms of knowledge maturing, e.g., some are good in the early phases, while others are good in the late phases – because their culture is more towards communication.

- **Collaboration and communication structures.** These are established practices of collaboration which do not need to be negotiated on every occasion. If there are regular team meetings where you can naturally bring up new ideas, this will be the forum for discussion. If there is no such meeting, or if this meeting is not for discussion, then you have first to create such a forum. Similarly, the quality of informal communication channels, both within and across organisations, has an impact on how knowledge maturing processes actually happen.

- **Shared practices.** This refers to work and business processes. Even more than collaboration and communication structures, they determine how everyday tasks are executed, they structure the division of labour etc. As a consequence, they are the primary frame of reference for knowledge maturing processes, particularly those concerned with knowledge how to do things.

6.1.3 Managerial Guidance

Managerial guidance for knowledge maturing is embedded in general management and leadership functions in organisations the purpose of which is the definition of organisational goals and the alignment of individual activities with those goals. Managerial guidance for knowledge maturing is thus interlinked with organisational goals, which typically implicitly or explicitly constitute a goal hierarchy, from very general and abstract to more specific, up to employee-level goals (as visible e.g., in management-by-objective approaches). Key performance indicators (KPIs) are typically used to measure to which degree goals have been reached.

In analogy to that, the knowledge maturing indicators from the previous section can be used to trace the effect of interventions into the organisation with respect to knowledge maturing. We can make use of the indicators at different levels, depending on the level of the intervention. From the discussion in the previous section, it has become clear that these indicators are context-dependent heuristics to approximate actual knowledge maturing processes. This means that from the presented collection and based on the identified underlying assumptions, a reasonable set has to be selected and often refined to match the needs of a company and the requirements and context of a specific situation.

But what can management interventions look like? We could identify the following:

- **Setting goals and thus giving priority.** Without prescribing what to do or what to change, management can influence maturing processes through setting goals to be achieved and/or giving priority to certain maturing activities or processes. The first aspect stimulates change with a certain organisational effect, thus guides the creativity towards a certain goal. The second changes the allocation of resources and could address the (most frequently) mentioned barriers of (1) lack of time and (2) low awareness of the value and benefit, such as creating a working group with a clear mission linked to organisational goals.

- **Shape work environment and work organisation.** Interventions could also include changing the work environment and/or the work organisation. In the first case, this refers, e.g., to improving, or deploying tools for maturing support; in the second case, this refers to division of labour, the conscious, goal-oriented shaping of communities-of-practice and business processes.

- **Organise and coach learning processes.** Interventions can take place both on an individual or on a collective level. On an individual level, this encompasses typical human resource development activities aimed at individual development (through trainings, coaching etc.). On a collective level, this is also about organisational learning, e.g., establishing reflective practice, continuous improvement processes, but also more local aspects, such as interventions into group processes.

6.1.4 Seeding – Evolutionary Growth – Reseeding

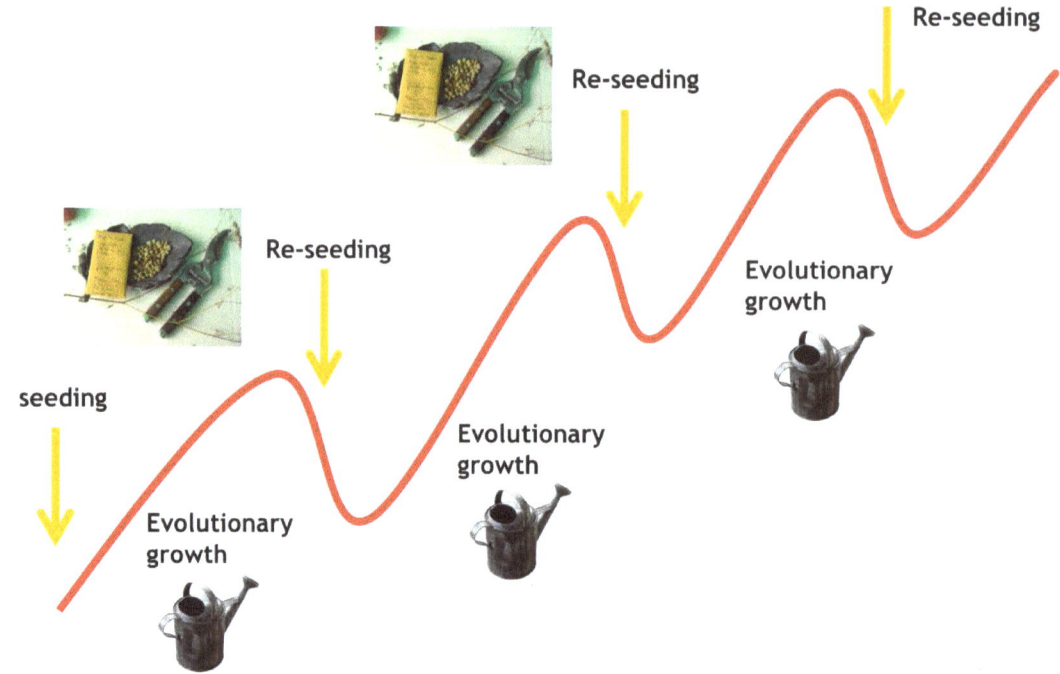

A closer look how to balance guidance with bottom-up initiatives has shown that the theory of Seeding, Evolutionary Growth and Reseeding, (SER) [Fischer et al. 2001] is suitable here. The SER model describes how complex systems evolve out of an initial seed (units, structure, and capabilities) and through the use of combination, analysis and change tools by many diverse users. Community activity leads to evolutionary, undirected (and often confusing) growth of the original units, structures and capabilities. At some point in time, the evolved system needs to be reseeded in order to be kept manageable. This reseeding can happen in a form of consolidation and negotiation processes in which the variety of units, structures, and capabilities are pruned and consolidated.

Seeding initiates the maturing process and leads into the evolutionary growth phase. At some point in the process, decisions have to be made. One alternative is to reseed the current maturity step. This would involve cleaning and pruning the current status and giving additional impulses so that the group can refocus.

For an example consider the maturity phase 'distributing in communities'. First a community 'space' is seeded with the initial idea or topic. This involves creating an initial knowledge structure together with its knowledge units and their capabilities and characteristics. In order to enable evolutionary growth this community environment needs to be equipped with means (tools) for combination, analysis, and change of the structures and the units themselves. Such tools allow the diverse users to combine knowledge units to build (increasingly complex) knowledge structures and to change the knowledge units themselves according to their needs. Analysis tools enable the community to monitor and guide its activities. If the development of the topic reaches a certain level, the decision whether to take the topic to the level of formalizing has to be made. If the development of the topic stagnates, reseeding might be an option. This includes pruning the current knowledge base, introducing new ideas, knowledge elements or people into the community or changing the topic.

6.2 IN-DEPTH CONSIDERATIONS AND SCIENTIFIC CONTEXT

6.2.1 Guidance concepts in related fields

There are a number of similar concepts that relate to the term guidance, e.g.,

- *governance*: specifying the decision rights and accountability framework to encourage desirable behavior (Weill and Ross, 2004),
- *influence*: generally meaning that a system, e.g., an agent, can impact on another system's behaviour, e.g., another agent's, behavior (Cialdini, 2008),
- *intervention*: meaning an external agent systematically attempts to induce a desirable change of a system by applying a specified set of instruments,
- *scaffolding*: describing a form of cognitive learning support to help learners to solve tasks that they would not be able to solve on their own (Wood et al., 1976). This support takes place within the learner's Zone of Proximal Development (ZPD, Vygotsky, 1978), i.e., the zone between what the learner currently is capable of and the potential developmental level which can be achieved through guidance and support.
- *leadership*: comprises among others traits (Eysenck, 1992), attributes, styles (Lewin et al., 1939), behaviour of leaders in organizing collectives of people to pursue a joint goal,
- *management*: comprises analysis, decision, evaluation and control (Ansoff 1966) and, with respect to change, creation, adaption, and coping with change (Leontiades, 1982)

The analysis of definitions of terms that are related to guidance also supports a closer look at the dyad of guide and guided system. For example from **leadership theories**, we can learn that personality traits, attributes, styles and behaviour of the guide with respect to the guided system will impact on the relationship between the two and the extent to which the guided system will feel inclined to accept the guide's influence on the decision taken by the guided system. In case of supervision/subordinate and thus hierarchical relationships between guide and guided system, the view that guidance leaves the decision with the guided system can be overlaid by a postulated congruency between the goals of the guided systems and those of the guide.

From **management theories** we can learn that also guides might pursue a part of the management cycle of analysis of the situation, decision of whom, what and how to guide as well as evaluation of what happened to the guided system afterwards. From governance theories, we can learn that implementing and using MATURE concepts and software tools might require or, if not considered appropriately, simply bring with it changes to the decision rights and accountability framework in which decisions concerning knowledge maturing will be taken.

From **theories on the psychology of persuasion**, we can learn that guidance can influence human behaviour by exploiting "weaknesses" of the guided system so that it commits to the guide's goals which might even contradict the goals of the guided system. From psychological theories on intervention, we can learn that guidance might even become a more or less systematic intervention into the guided system with the more or less explicit goal of change in order to prevent or to resolve a disorder or to confine its negative consequences.

From **scaffolding** and the **Zone of Proximal Development**, we can learn that when approaching guidance from an individual learning perspective guidance should be (a) temporary (i.e., learners should be on their own again when they have learnt to master a task or problem) and (b) within the Zone of Proximal Development (i.e., it should be outside the current capabilities of the learner, but still within reach) to avoid a patronizing effect and mental overload – both of which stifle motivation. In our view, this can be generalized to a team level, where ZPD would be defined on the collective level.

6.2.2 Guidance Levels

As much as these terms can be seen on varying levels as the object system might be a single individual, a group, a project team, a department, a division, an organization or even a group or a network of organizations, as much guidance can be exerted on varying levels of intervention. However, with respect to the MATURE concepts and software, the following guidance levels are of primary importance:

- **knowledge maturing capabilities**: guidance means here that participants, organizational or technical infrastructures of an organisation as a guided system are influenced with the aim that this organisation can improve its general capabilities useful for improved knowledge maturing, independent of a specific domain, topic, project, process or other concrete initiative in which these capabilities should be applied.

- **knowledge maturing process type**: guidance means here that participants, organizational or technical infrastructures are influenced with the aim that the process of knowledge maturing is improved in general, as laid out in the knowledge maturing phase model, i.e. independent of a specific domain or topic,

- **knowledge maturing process instance**: guidance means here that participants, organizational or technical infrastructures are influenced with the aim that a specific process of knowledge maturing is improved, i.e. concerning maturing of knowledge on a specific domain or topic,

- **knowledge maturing activity type:** guidance means here that participants, organizational or technical infrastructures are influenced with the aim that a knowledge maturing activity is generally improved, e.g., reflect on and refine work practices or processes or find people with particular knowledge or expertise.

- **knowledge maturing activity instance**: guidance means here that participants, organizational or technical infrastructures are influenced with the aim that a specific knowledge maturing activity is improved, e.g., reflect on and refine work practices or processes or find people with particular knowledge or expertise concerning knowledge on a specific domain or topic.

From this categorization, it becomes easier to distinguish between different forms of guidance. The more general levels (general capability, process types, and activity type) are typically the target of tool support or structural interventions as they need to have a generic effect, while direct human interventions are also effective on a less abstract level (like giving advice).

6.2.3 Guidance activities

Based on an in-depth analysis of cases of companies that were particularly successful in supporting knowledge maturing, the following guidance activities have been identified:

1. **Provide feedback.** This refers to external input on the progress and development. It can be based on an assessment, but could be also a form of information, e.g., how one's own ideas and contributions are used by others.

2. **Respond.** Responding to inquiries from others is a form of guidance. This does not necessarily include recommendations (can be also a response to a question without any opinion part).

3. **Recommend, suggest & advice.** This activity comprises various forms of influencing the direction of development where a peer, a more senior counterpart, or a superior recommends changing direction, using certain artefacts, executing certain actions.

4. **Irritate & challenge.** Here, the guiding entity does not suggest a certain route, but rather provides a possibility for reflection by challenging the status quo and the associated assumptions and beliefs.

5. **Structure & organize**. This can be a preparatory guidance activities (seeding), but also a form of reseeding where the knowledge area or certain artefacts are structured to reduce the complexity. The structure itself as the result of the guidance activity also has a guiding effect.

6. **Make aware.** In this activity, the guided person is made aware of new or changed developments, existence of other items outside his current perspective, the need or potential for action in a certain area. This is typically done through informing, or peripheral awareness facilities. In contrast to recommendation, it is non-judgmental.

7. **Encourage.** This refers to targeting at the motivation of individuals, particularly to overcome uncertainty and doubts associated with new fields. This encouragement can be on a peer level, but can be also effective in a hierarchical setting.

8. **Evaluate & assess results**. Within this activity, results (or partial results) are more closely examined by the guiding entity. While it usually is also a form of feedback, it is based on a more thorough assessment.

9. **Coordinate.** Particularly for managing the complexity of parallel knowledge maturing processes, coordination is an important guidance activities as it might create links between different strands and avoid duplication of efforts. Coordination can be personal or structural; in the latter case coordination is institutionalized through team and collaboration structures.

10. **Create opportunities.** This is typically not an activity that targets at the individual knowledge maturing process instance, but it rather refers to decisions like giving free time, institutionalizing regular meetings, introducing tools like new collaboration platforms etc. that represent enablers for effective knowledge maturing processes. It could also refer to changing cultural conditions that block opportunities as part of an organizational development process.

11. **Reward.** This refers to giving someone credit for an achievement in the past. This is more typical for hierarchical structures to signal appreciation of the work done so far. This can have a positive motivational effect for future activities, and it

12. **Monitor activities & progress.** This refers to observing ongoing developments and can serve as a prerequisite for other guidance activities.

13. **Give legitimation.** This refers to an organizational activity which is particularly important for advancing from earlier phases of knowledge maturing to later phases – phases IV and V cannot be achieved without a form of legitimation. With legitimation, the organization signals that this activity is in line with organizational goals. It usually implies also that it is easier to get additional resources.

We can observe that for guidance activities we can distinguish between activities that are based on the organizational hierarchy and those based on peer influence. Guidance activities 1-8 are clearly independent of the company hierarchy, while the activities 10-13 are embedded into the hierarchical system of the organization. Activity 9 can be both, depending on the form of coordination. Coordination can happen in a self-organizing system, but it can be also the role of management.

A second observation is that some knowledge maturing activities are closely related to a guidance activity, such as *assess, verify & rate* and *evaluate & assess results*, *respond/provide feedback* and *communicate with people*, *structure & organize* and *reorganise information at individual or organisational level,* or *make aware* and *keep up-to-date with organisation-related knowledge*. The main distinction between the two that in case of guidance activities, the actor takes an external perspective on the knowledge maturing process while in the case of knowledge maturing activities, the actor forms part of the knowledge maturing process.

6.3 FURTHER READING

Kaschig, A., Maier, R., Sandow, A. & Schmidt, A. (Eds.) (2010). D1.2 - Results Of The Representative Study And Refined Conceptual Knowledge Maturing Model. Deliverable of the FP7 IP MATURE,, section 5.4.2, pp. 153-155, http://d.mature-ip.eu/D1.2

> *Conceptualization of guidance*

Kaschig, A., Maier, R., Sandow, A. & Schmidt, A. (Eds.) (2011). D1.3 Results of In-depth Case Studies, Recommendations and Final Knowledge Maturing Model. Deliverable of the FP7 IP MATURE, Section 5.3, pp. 97-102, and the case studies in section 4, http://d.mature-ip.eu/D1.3

> *Derivation of guidance activities from in-depth case studies, relating the concept of guidance to other disciplines*

Schmidt, Andreas, Hinkelmann, Knut, Ley, Tobias, Lindstaedt, Stefanie, Maier, Ronald, Riss, Uwe: Conceptual Foundations for a Service-oriented Knowledge and Learning Architecture: Supporting Content, Process and Ontology Maturing. In: Schaffert, Sebastian and Tochtermann, Klaus and Pellegrini, Tassilo (eds.): Networked Knowledge - Networked Media: Integrating Knowledge Management, New Media Technologies and Semantic Systems, Springer, 2009, pp. 79-94

> *The Seeding-Evolutionary Growth-Reseeding model and guidance*

7

Rethinking and Redefining Enterprise Systems

Knowledge Maturing changes the way we have to conceive enterprise systems. As knowledge maturing transcends many work activities, support for knowledge maturing needs to be integrated into those system and as a consequence fundamentally changes their underlying assumptions.

When we come to think about how to support such learning activities which form part of knowledge maturing processes, we discover that traditional tools and systems are woefully inadequate. Virtual learning environments (or, learning management systems) are far too focused on the administrative and formal aspects of guiding learning. Knowledge management systems are far too concentrated on the organizational scope, but do not adequately take into account the individual and community aspects of learning. What we rather need, are forms of learning support leverage the intrinsic motivation of employees to engage in collaborative learning activities, and combine it with a new form of organisational guidance. That requires a change in corporate attitude, or culture towards more participation: the organization needs to encourage the individual employee to bring in her ideas, to develop them with their peers, and the organization needs to take up those activities and guide their further development towards a shared goal. This more participatory perspective is now bringing to mind the fundamental change that knowledge workers have brought to the way people work. Instead of strict orders or work organizations, they need loose forms of coordination of a complex network of individuals towards strategic objectives.

7.1 COMPETENCE MANAGEMENT

Competence management systems are based on competence catalogues that are created by expert groups in long and expensive processes. However, these competence catalogues are only rarely updated and thus do not contain up-to-date emerging competencies. Furthermore, competence scales often suggest an accuracy for competence profiles that does not reflect the ambiguity of the underlying competence notions. As a consequence, most competence management approaches are perceived as administrative exercises with limited usefulness (Braun et al, 2012).

From a knowledge maturing perspective, these systems do not take into account the dynamic nature of competency notions as cultural constructs. This means: (i) the way of defining profiles must reflect the maturity of the respective competency notion, and (ii) broad participation must be possible to capture emerging topics that will eventually evolve into stable competence definitions.

The approach of MATURE was a lightweight approach based on collaborative tagging as a principle to gather the information about persons inside and outside the company (if and where relevant): individuals tag each other according to the topics they associate with this person. We call this 'people tagging'. In this way, we gain a collective review of existing skills and competencies. Knowledge can be shared and awareness strengthened within the organisational context around who knows what. This tagging information can then be used to search for persons to talk to in a particular situation. Moreover it can also be used for various other purposes. For instance, human resource development needs to have sufficient information about the needs and current capabilities of current employees to make the right decisions about training required. Our approach provides a clear indication on

- What type of expertise is needed?

- How much of the required expertise already exists within the organisation?

- Which gaps exist in specific skills and competencies?

This needs continuous development of a shared vocabulary (ontology). Competencies usually have an integrating function in the enterprise, bringing together strategic and operational levels, and human resources, and performance management aspects.so that these notions have to be shared by the whole organization (in the ideal case): in consequence we cannot do this without a shared vocabulary – a shared vocabulary which the employees evolve in its usage, i.e. during the tagging or search process. With our tools, the employees can tag each other with concepts from the shared vocabulary. In the case they want to tag with a topic the existing ontology concepts do not cover (e.g. because the topic is too new or specific), the employees can adapt an existing concept or just use a new term, without an agreed meaning. These new terms are automatically added to the shared vocabulary as "prototypical concepts", reflecting the fact that it's not clear yet how they relate to the existing concepts. The users can then remove the new terms from the "prototypical concepts" container and integrate them into the vocabulary and add additional information. This results in an "ontology maturing process" that is a specialization of a knowledge maturing process.

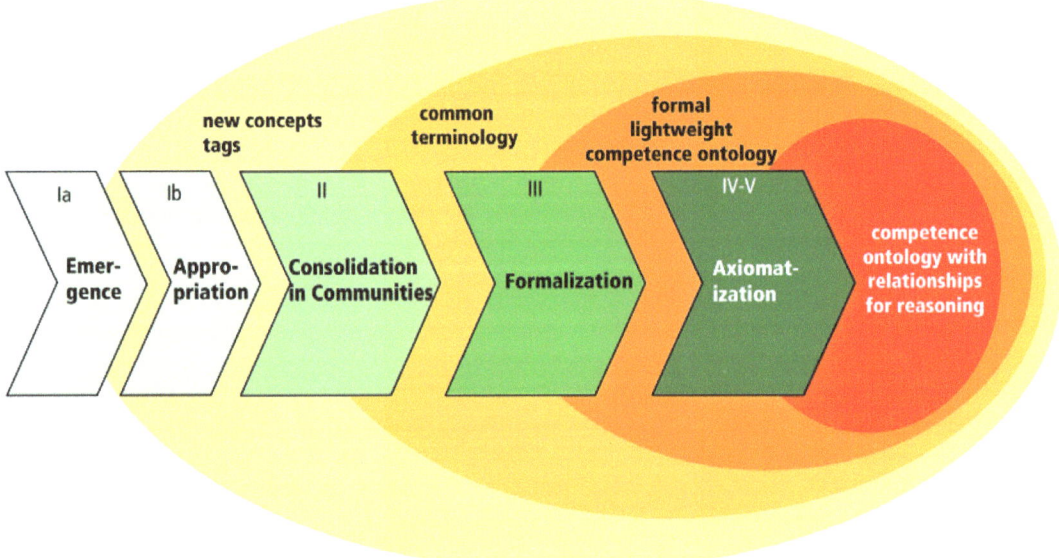

Figure 17: Ontology Maturing

7.2 BUSINESS PROCESS MANAGEMENT

Business process support systems are based on highly formalized business process models. A common problem is that these process models are not appropriate for the situations encountered in daily work practice so that employees do not comply, create shortcuts or similar. In most cases, the issue is not that the process model is wrong. In the light of the knowledge maturing model, the underlying problem is that the actual knowledge is not mature enough to be specified in a process model.

As a consequence, (i) the processes should be carefully selected with respect to the maturity of the underlying, and even more important (ii) knowledge management needs to find ways how to ensure that formalized processes can be continuously further developed in response to changes in the environments that requires evolution of the underlying process knowledge.

Furthermore, similar to competence management, process descriptions need to be continuously evolved to the most appropriate level of maturity. The following table explains the respective phases.

	Flexible direct enactment	Descriptive pattern-support	Prescriptive pattern-support	Strict process models
User perspective	Pros: Flexible performance in new situations Cons: No user support	Pros: Benefit from existing experiences Cons: Challenge to locate patterns matching needs	Pros: Clear guidance on relevant deviation options Cons: Fewer deviation options	Pros: Strict guidance for core processes Cons: No deviation for new situations
Organisation perspective	Pros: Support performance in new situations; *opportunities for user support* Cons: No standardisation or control	Pros: Evolve org knowledge; *opportunities for user support* Cons: Lack control over deviations	Pros: Standardise org knowledge for relatively stable processes; control deviation options Cons: Some modelling / approval	Pros: Standardise core org processes Cons: Expensive, upfront modelling
Deviation support	Everything is ad hoc and user-driven	Support direct enactment with patterns	Deviations restricted to approved options	No deviation
Open issues	Can some user support be provided?	Are deviations from selected pattern controlled? Any guidance or constraints on pattern options?	Are deviations within restricted patterns controlled? Do we need a fallback strategy for new situations?	

7.3   CONTENT MANAGEMENT

Document-centric systems have been viewed as the key instrument to knowledge management in the past generation of knowledge management systems. While documents can be useful for distributing knowledge to a large audience, they are only an efficient approach if the knowledge represented in them has the same maturity. It is comparably much less useful to document ideas that are too heavily contextualized. Also we need different types of functionalities for different phases: the earlier phases need easy collaboration, while the latter phases are more about quality control. A one-size-fits-all approach is not possible, although it would be desirable to have a single system, also to ensure continuity.

7.4   FURTHER READING

Braun, Simone, Kunzmann, Christine, Braun, Simone (2012): People Tagging – An Enterprise Social Media Approach to Competence Management. International Journal on Knowledge and Learning (in press)

Description of the knowledge maturing approach to competence management

References

The references can be found in the underlying deliverables that are listed in the "Further Reading" section.

Imprint

This whitepaper report summarizes the results of the MATURE Integrating Project (http://mature-ip.eu), which was co-funded by the European Commission under FP7, and is intended to provide easy access to the wealth of result that have been produced in four years of research. For the matter of conciseness, scientific references are only included to a limited extent. Full references and more elaborate discussions can be found in the underlying deliverables that are mentioned in the respective chapters.

For more information: http://knowledge-maturing.com

Contact: andreas.schmidt@knowledge-maturing.com

Bibliographical information / cite as:

Andreas Schmidt, Christine Kunzmann (eds.) (2012):
Knowledge Maturing – Creating Learning Rich Workplaces for Agile Organizations
Report. http://knowledge-maturing.com/files/whitepaper.pdf

www.ingramcontent.com/pod-product-compliance
Lightning Source LLC
Chambersburg PA
CBHW051052180526
45172CB00002B/611